84B20

Jim McJunkin

Published by:
    2nd Tier Publishing
    13501 Ranch Road 12, Ste 103
    Wimberley, TX 78676

Copyright © 2014 by Jim McJunkin

ISBN 978-0-9894642-6-0

Thanks to Beth McJunkin, Don Minick, Dan Gauthier and Shiila Safer for making this book possible. Also, thanks to the US Army, and whoever designated 84B20 as my military occupational specialty.

Condolences to all the civilians whose lives were rendered collateral damage due to military conflict.

In 1980 I answered an advertisement in an art magazine. A group of artists from Chicago were trying to organize an exhibition by Vietnam veterans concerning their wartime experiences. The short version of a long story is that my photographs were accepted into the show, which was more successful than any of us could imagine. I had never seen an art exhibit with more impact, or one that produced such an emotional response.

The Vietnam Veterans Arts Group (VVAG) grew from fewer than twenty artists that participated in the first show to over a hundred Vietnam veterans from around the world. The art includes pieces that were created in Vietnam and pieces that were created as a cathartic response to the Vietnam war experience. They have been exhibited in major museums and universities around the world. In the United States, VVAG art has been displayed in the House and Senate chambers, and various presidential libraries.

In 1996, the VVAG was awarded a large building in downtown Chicago that was renovated into the National Vietnam War Museum.

In 1998 The VVAG produced an excellent book, *Vietnam, Reflexes and Reflections*, by Abrams Publishing.

Over the years I have met many of the VVAG artists, guys that saw and did things that will haunt them forever. Their art is an emotional expression of thoughts and memories. One of those men was a prisoner of war from 1968–1973. During that time he was kept in tiger cages in the jungle, the infamous Hanoi Hilton Prison in North Vietnam, and various prison camps in China. Some of his pen and ink drawings are hard to look at.

Over the years I have heard a good many stories, confessions and nightmares. I usually keep quiet during those discussions because in comparison, my Vietnam experiences belong in a children's book. I don't have a problem with that. It was my good fortune. My level of commitment to a war that killed and wounded so many young men is more problematic, but even that was an honest reaction. It is history now, and this is the way it unfolded.

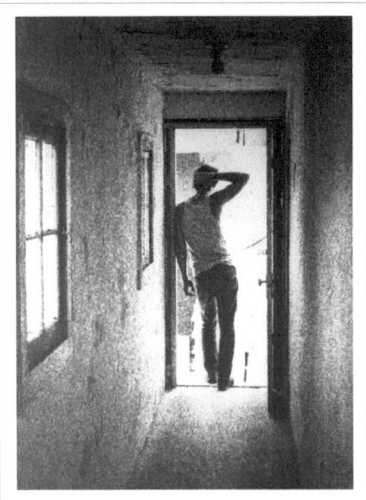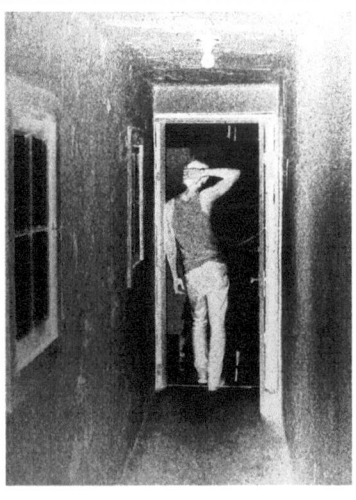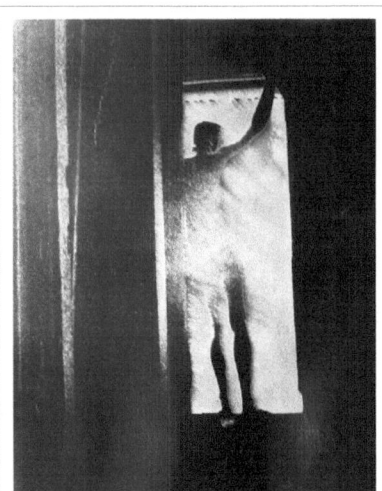

My dad loaned me his 35mm Voightlander camera so I could take pictures of my friends. I wanted the images for a high school art project. They were to be studies that I could reproduce on canvas. The final project did not have to be an accurate reproduction, and my intent was to paint my friends into some sort of fantasy world.

It was my last year at George Washington high school, in Denver, Colorado. Salvador Dali was the artist I most wanted to emulate, but psychedelia, pop, and optical art were beginning to insinuate themselves into the art world, especially in the form of album covers and concert posters.

The Voightlander slowly became a means of altering reality, which seemed important at the time. I learned how to make multiple exposures, and experimented with special effects films like infrared, and high contrast Kodalith. Later, when I was learning to process and print my images, I made paper negatives that infused a fiber pattern into the picture. It was photo-magic for the sake of art. I tried scratching, warping, and burning certain negatives, all in an effort to make the world more bizarre.

It would not take long for me to realize that "the times really were a changing." The summer between high school and college was a series of parties, music and drugs. The hippie revolution was in full swing, and I embraced it. Denver was exuding a circus atmosphere that made absurdity easy to photograph.

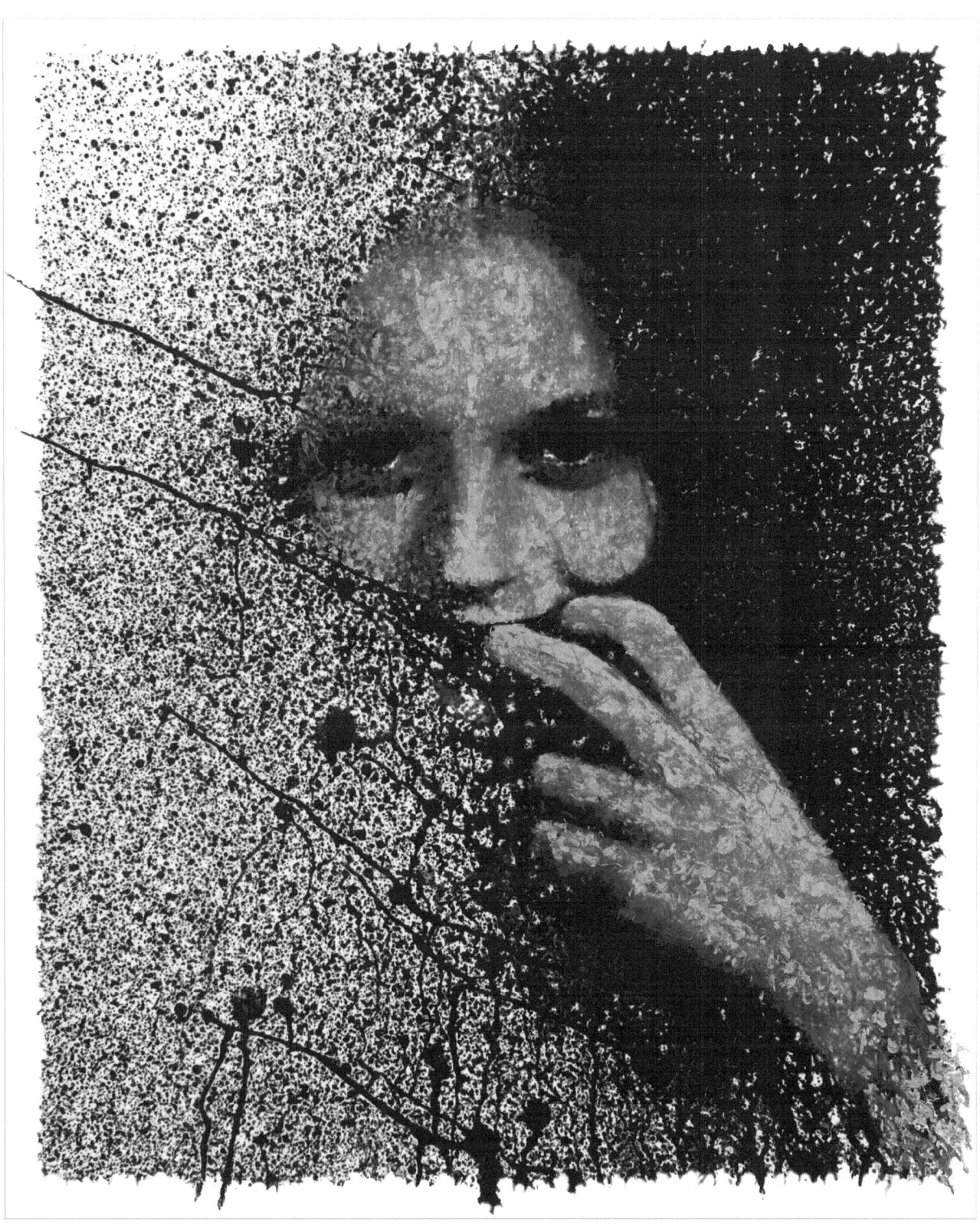

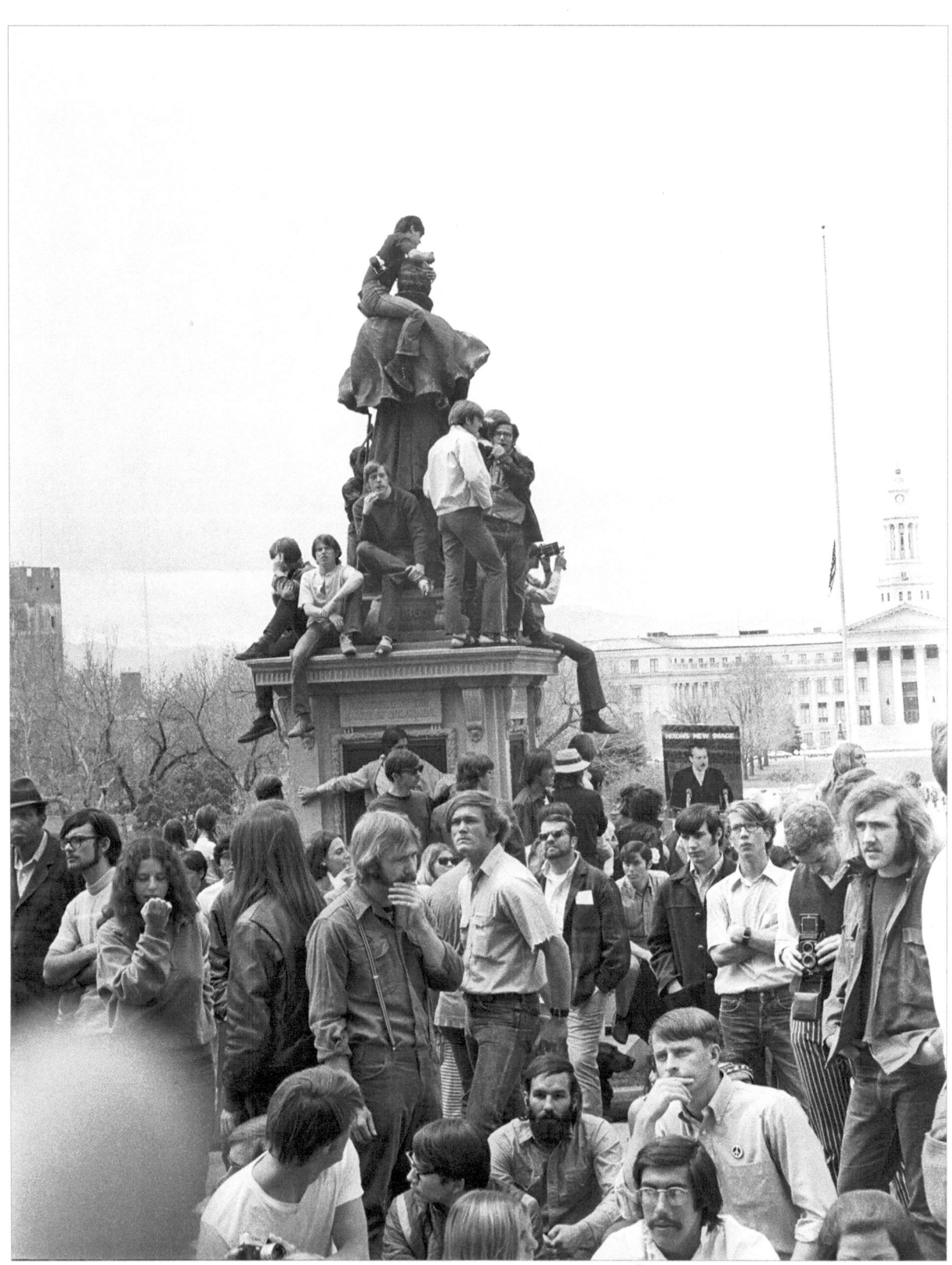

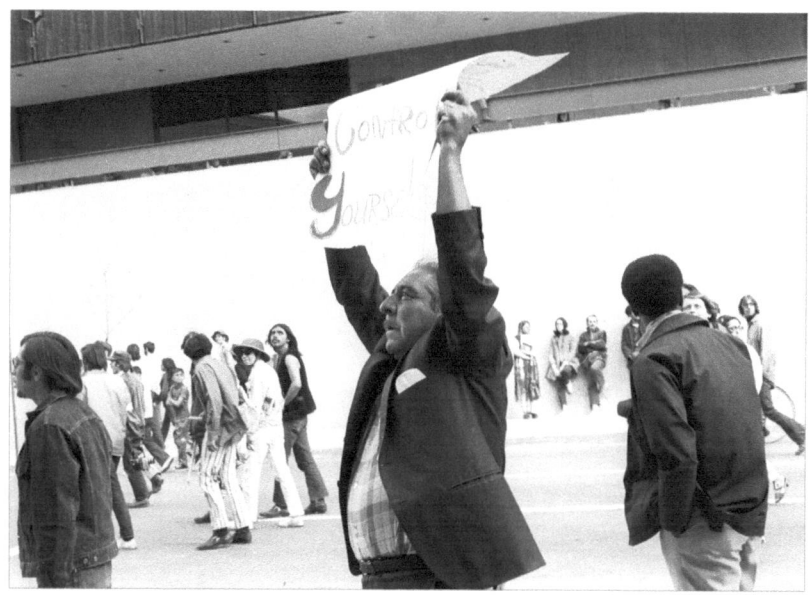

In 1968, having recently seen a movie about a photographer who does well with the opposite sex (*Blow-Up*), and thinking photography might be a cool thing to do, I bought a 35mm camera. I was an art major at the time, primarily working with paint on canvas and slowly coming to the realization that my talents in that medium might be limited. My ideas for paintings did not come easily, and when the canvas was done it usually resembled somebody else's work.

Using a camera began to seem like a more natural form of expression and the results were practically instantaneous. Best of all, the images were my own. It would be years before I tried to emulate other photographers work, and years after that before I realized it was a mistake. In the summer of 1968, in Denver, Colorado there was a steady stream of interesting scenes. It was just a matter of separating the still photographs from everyday life.

I used my camera at a couple of anti-war rallies, and carried it with a sense of purpose. It felt like a special ticket to the event. Most of the people were there to stop the war, an admirable cause that I was in total agreement with. Others were on hand because it was a happening, an outpouring of humanity that seemed strange even for the era. I would have gone for either reason. The draft board was closing in and my opposition to the war was at least as personal as it was philosophical. I photographed the events not for a higher purpose, but because it seemed like the thing to do.

The basics of photography came easy, and I quickly learned to keep my fingers away from the front of the lens. The camera became a motivator and a mask, and I began to collect pictures of events that happened around me.

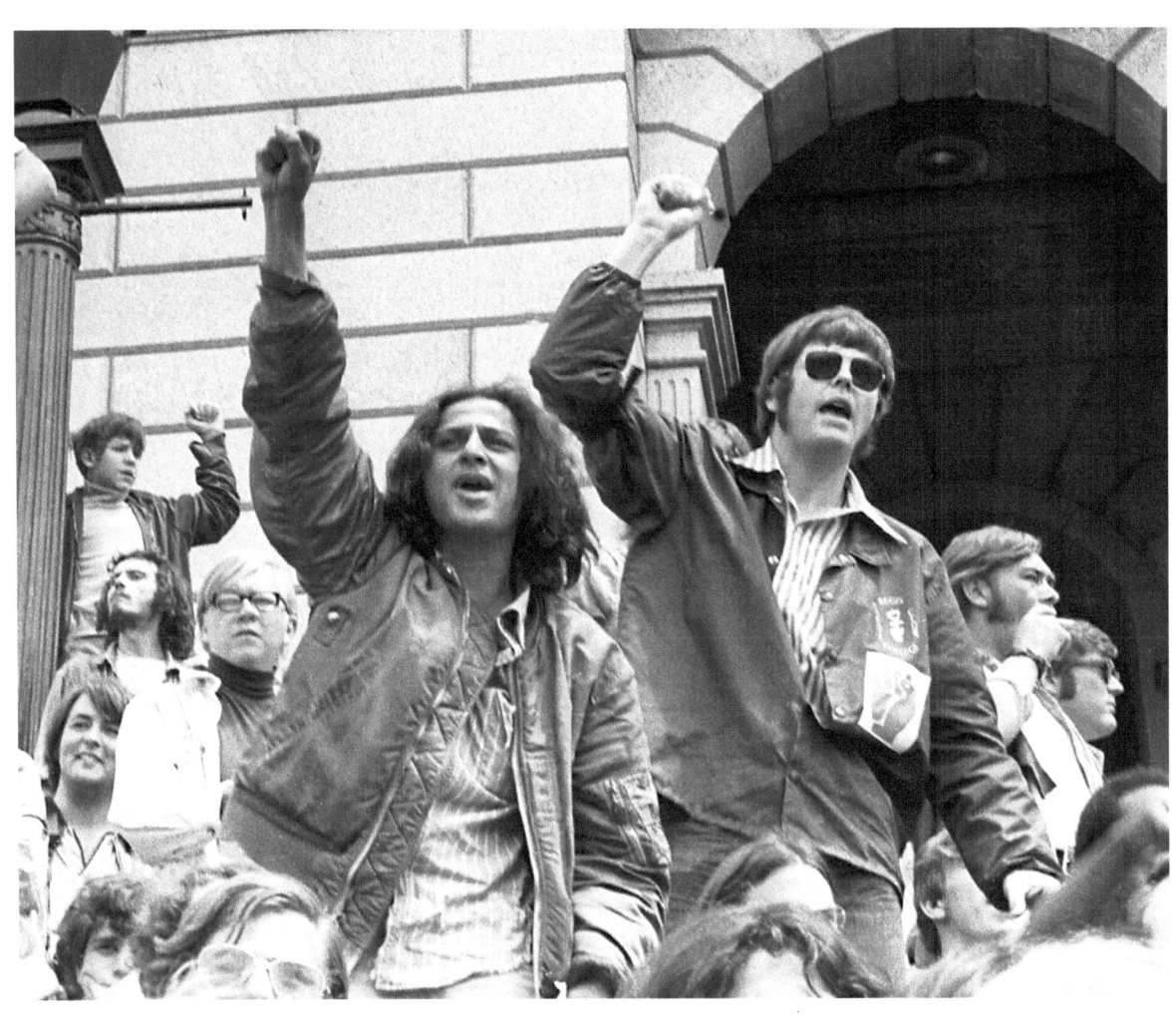

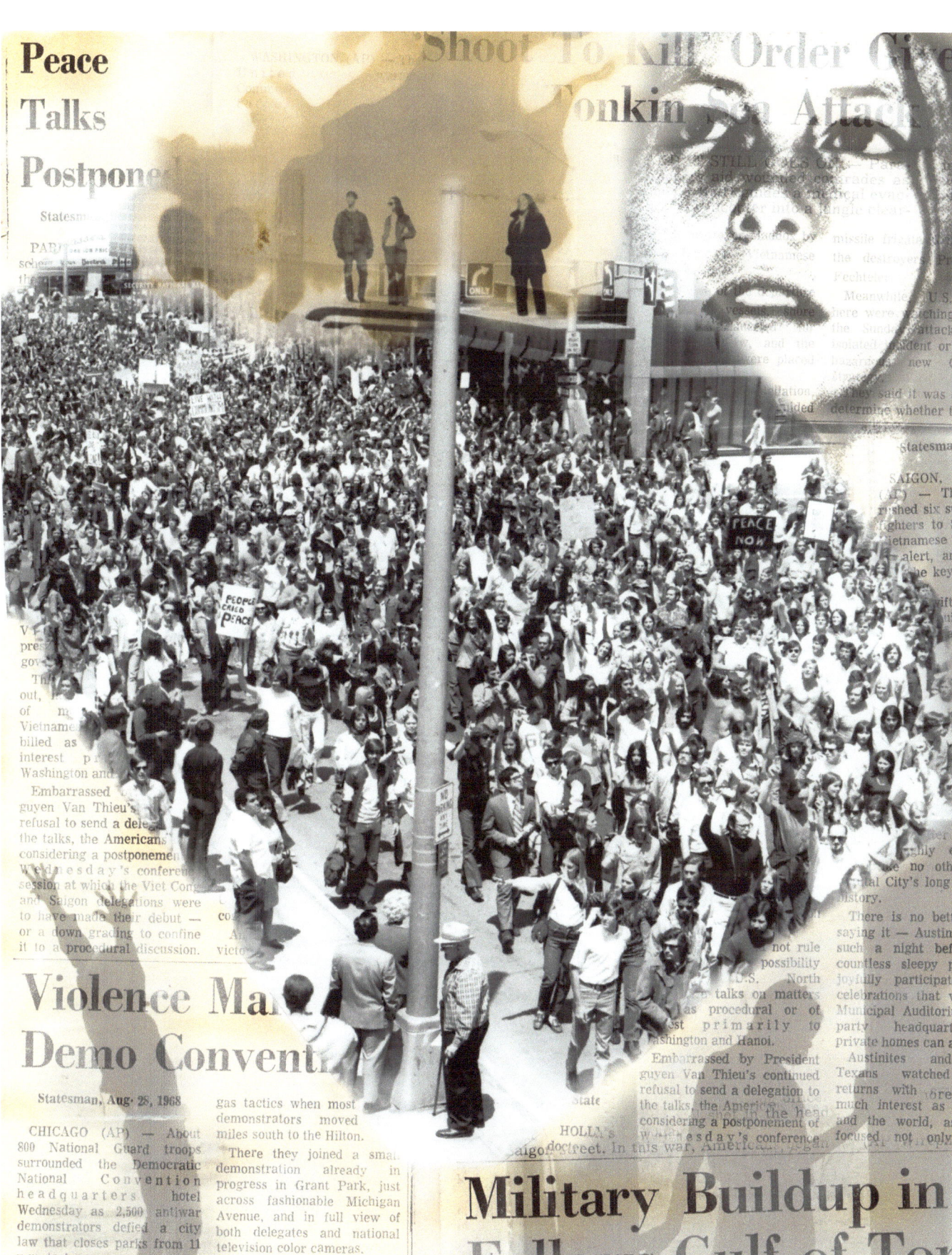

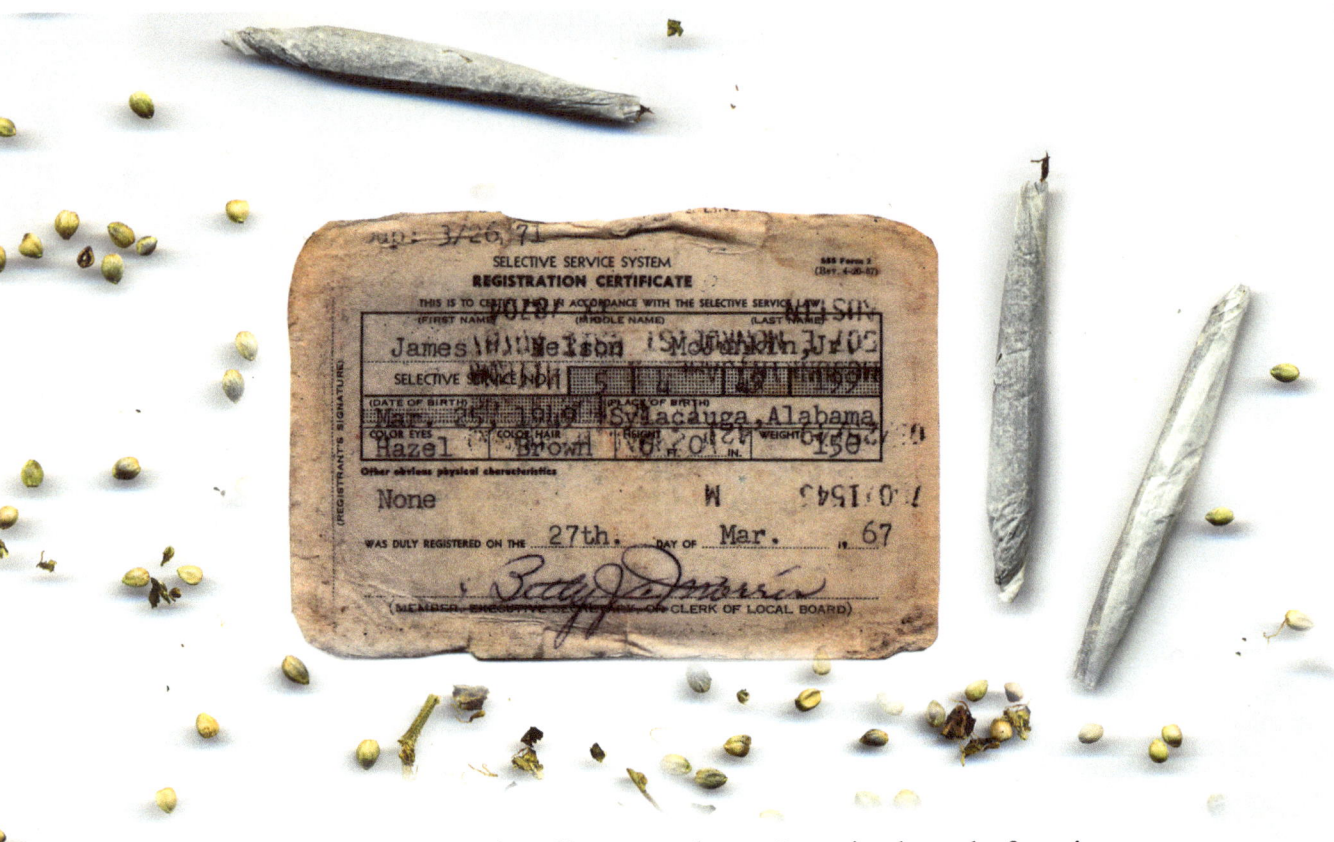

After some erratic college attendance, I received my draft notice. It was rumored that people who voluntarily joined the Army were less likely to go to Vietnam than those who were drafted; so I enlisted for two years. As a last act of defiance and desperation I listed professional photographer as my current source of employment and job preference on the enlistment form.

In June of 1969 I was sent to Fort Campbell, Kentucky for basic training. My attitude was contrary to the cohesive spirit the Army was trying to instill and one night I went AWOL with another soldier. The military police chased us through a cornfield and caught my partner. I managed to get away and hitch hiked back to Denver, Colorado, where it became apparent that life as a fugitive could be much worse than two years in the Army.

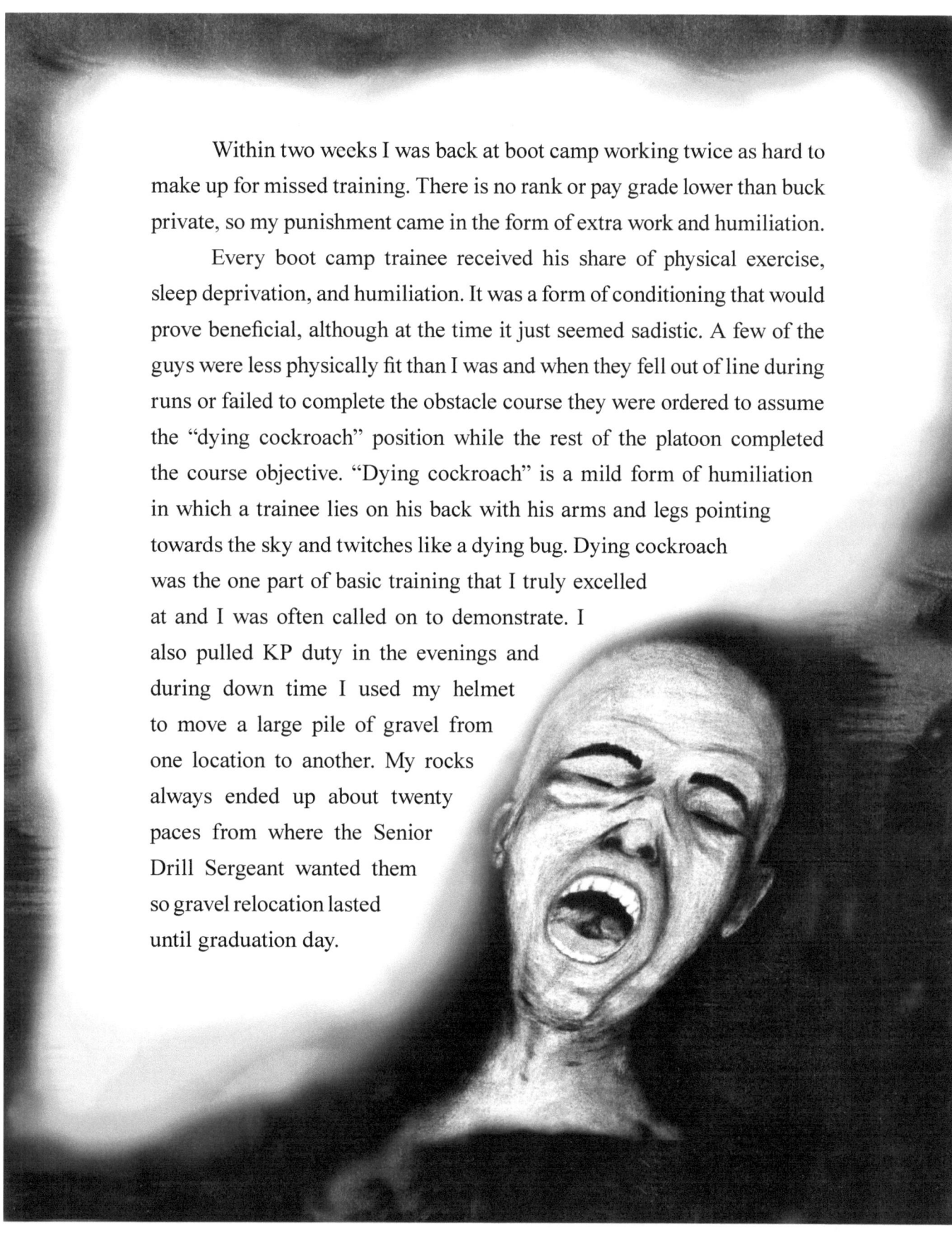

Within two weeks I was back at boot camp working twice as hard to make up for missed training. There is no rank or pay grade lower than buck private, so my punishment came in the form of extra work and humiliation.

Every boot camp trainee received his share of physical exercise, sleep deprivation, and humiliation. It was a form of conditioning that would prove beneficial, although at the time it just seemed sadistic. A few of the guys were less physically fit than I was and when they fell out of line during runs or failed to complete the obstacle course they were ordered to assume the "dying cockroach" position while the rest of the platoon completed the course objective. "Dying cockroach" is a mild form of humiliation in which a trainee lies on his back with his arms and legs pointing towards the sky and twitches like a dying bug. Dying cockroach was the one part of basic training that I truly excelled at and I was often called on to demonstrate. I also pulled KP duty in the evenings and during down time I used my helmet to move a large pile of gravel from one location to another. My rocks always ended up about twenty paces from where the Senior Drill Sergeant wanted them so gravel relocation lasted until graduation day.

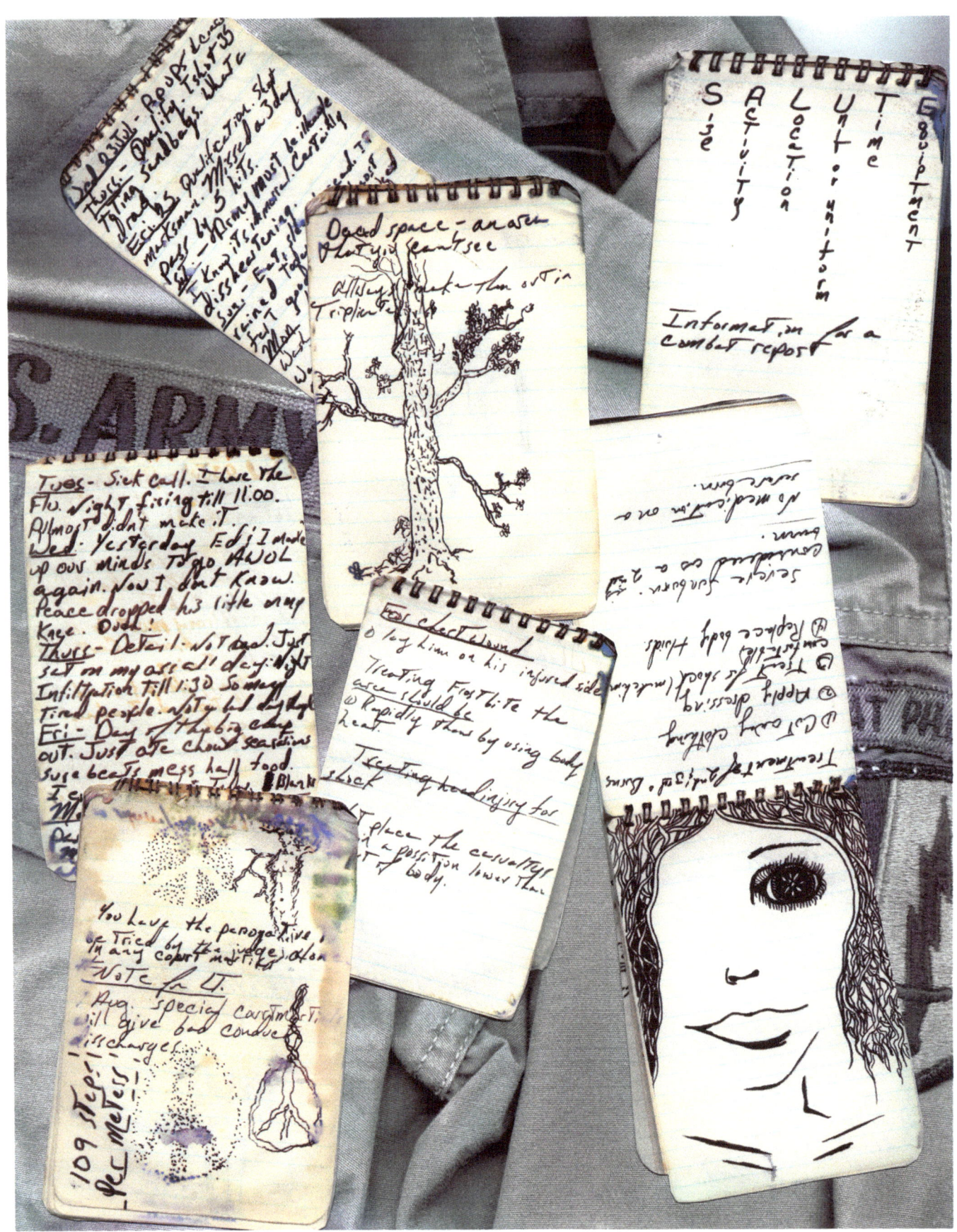

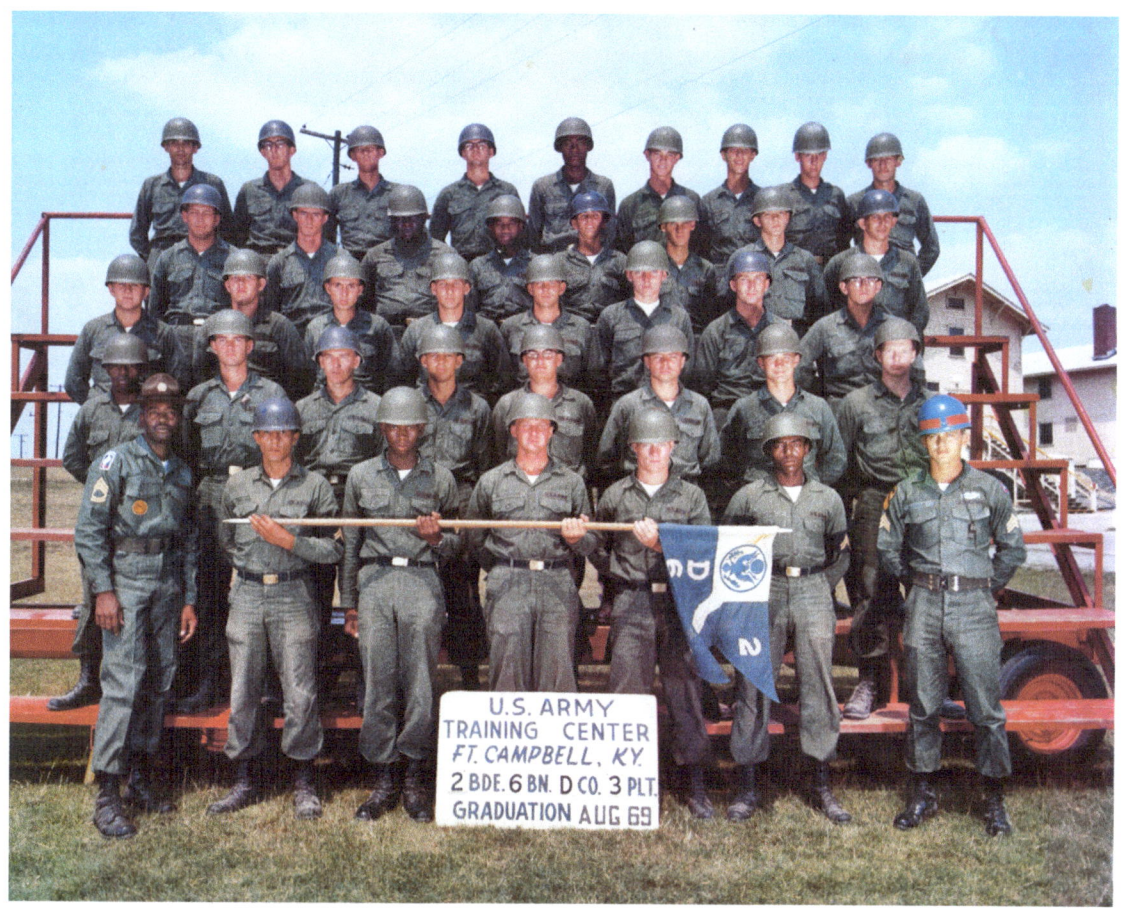

U.S. ARMY
TRAINING CENTER
FT. CAMPBELL, KY.
2 BDE. 6 BN. D CO. 3 PLT.
GRADUATION AUG 69

     This group portrait was taken on basic training graduation day. I'm on the top row, under the fourth helmet from the right. Our Senior Drill Sergeant is on the bottom row, far left. He once told me that the only reason he did not beat the crap out of me was that he already had fourteen congressional investigations pending for previous trainee beatings and I was not worth another. Some of the things he said were ludicrous, but the way he said them made me a believer.

     When our graduation ceremony was over the Senior Drill Sergeant read our MOS', (military occupational specialties), from a cryptic looking document. Most of the guys were 11B; riflemen, en route to Vietnam. My MOS was 84B20; still photographer, and my next duty station was Colorado Springs, Colorado.

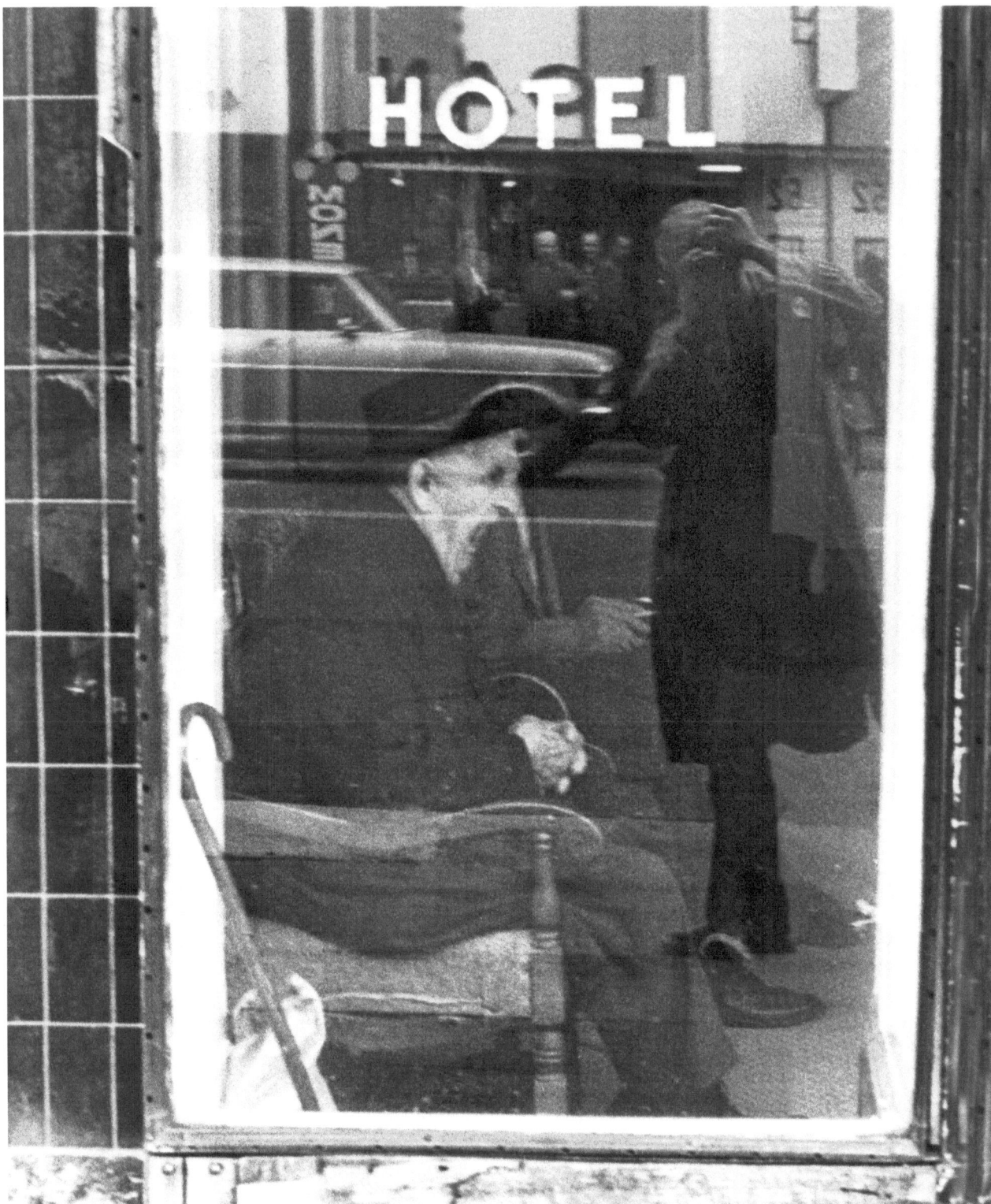

As a form of on the job training I became a photographers assistant, shooting award ceremonies, and learning to process and print film. A desire to learn the craft, and a severe attitude adjustment helped me assume the role of the ideal stateside soldier. Snappy salutes and a courteous manner made life easier, and assisted in my rise through the ranks in short order. My new persona had more to do with survival than anything else, but an unintended consequence was that I was allowed to check out an assortment of small to large format cameras from the base photo lab. I was also allowed to use the lab for personal work after hours. Photography became an obsession and I settled in to what could have been a dream assignment.

One night I was at an off-base party where the air was thick with marijuana smoke. The cops came in the front door and busted everybody except me. I just happened to be in the kitchen, close enough to the back door to exit the house, jump a fence and get away. I vaulted a few more fences, hid behind some bushes for an hour or two, and made my way back to base before sunup.

Monday morning two OSI officers came to the photo lab where I was working and took me away. Some girl at the party had turned me in. I denied everything, but they found some rolling papers and enough loose marijuana in a shirt pocket to analyze as cannabis. I was guilty as charged and busted from Spec. 4th class back to Pvt. 1st class. My duty station was changed to Vietnam.

I shipped out of the states from San Francisco after spending some time walking around the city taking pictures. This window reflection is one of the last images I made before leaving the United States.

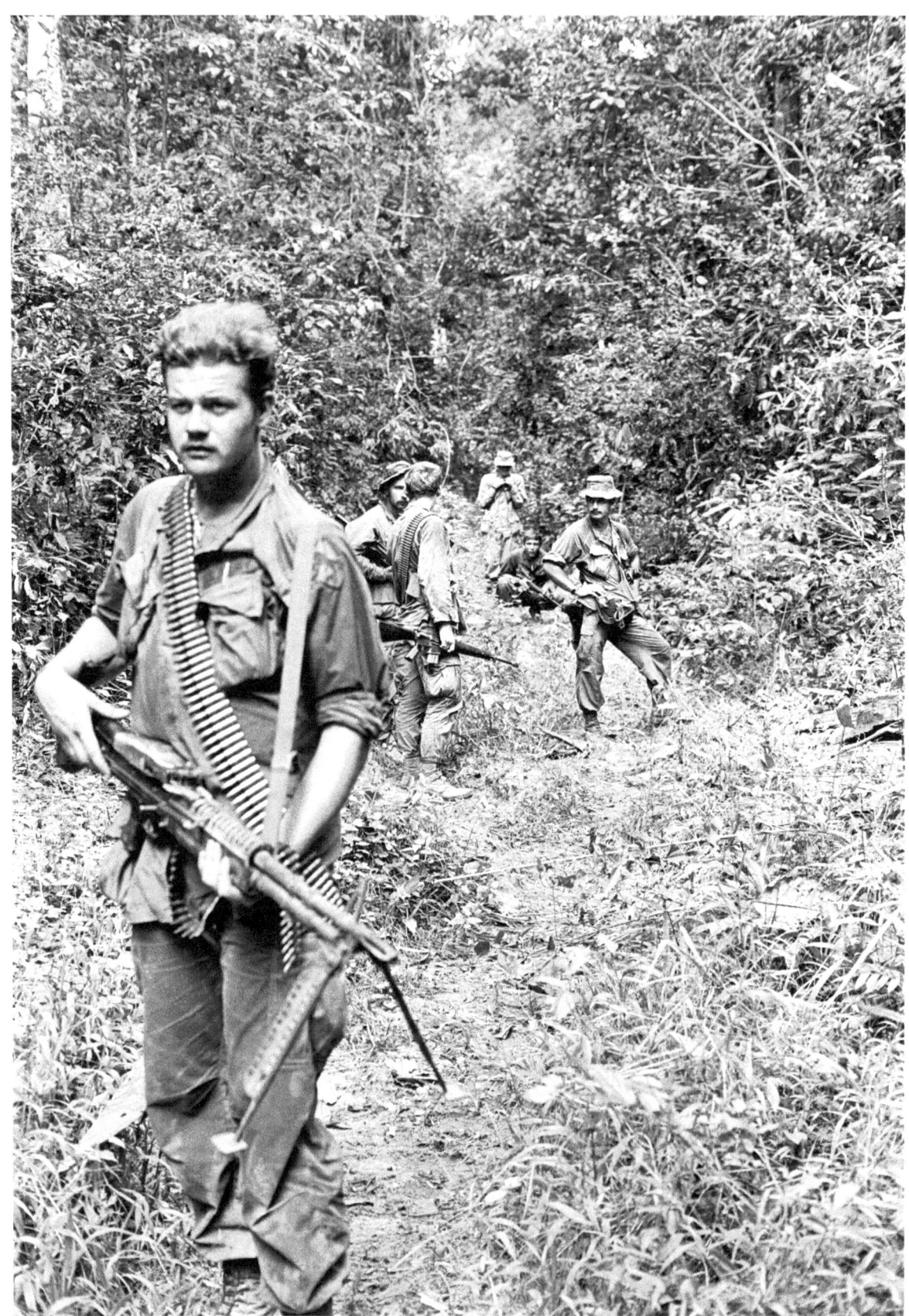

By late 1970, when I arrived in Vietnam, the character of the war had changed. The catalyst had been the Tet offensive of 1968, which practically decimated the Viet Cong, but galvanized American opposition. Now there were bigger and better organized demonstrations in the US and many of those demonstrators were being drafted and sent to Vietnam. Some of them showed up with bad attitudes and a penchant for drugs, which were available in surplus.

US involvement was gradually winding down and one of the most noticeable changes was that US troops went into the field in smaller numbers. Most enemy contact amounted to ambushes and firefights. It was a waiting game for soldiers on both sides of the conflict so the firefights were often the result of chance encounters and the ambushes tended to be automatic, (rig a trail with claymores and collect the bodies in the morning).

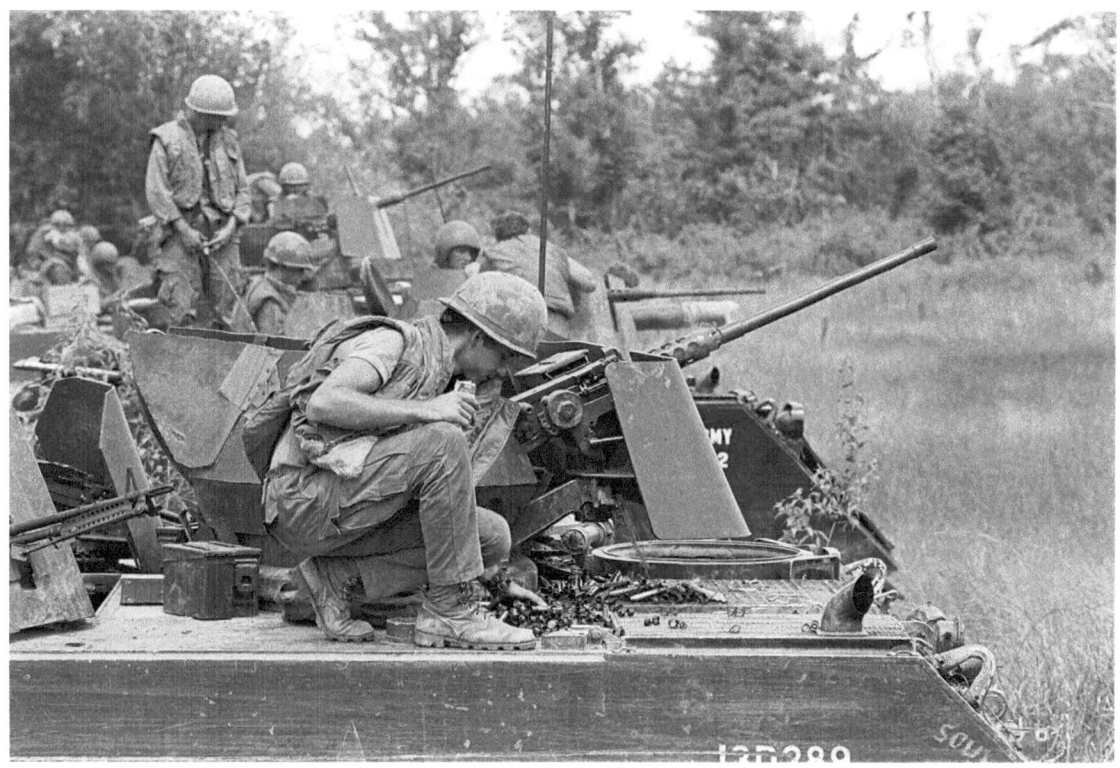

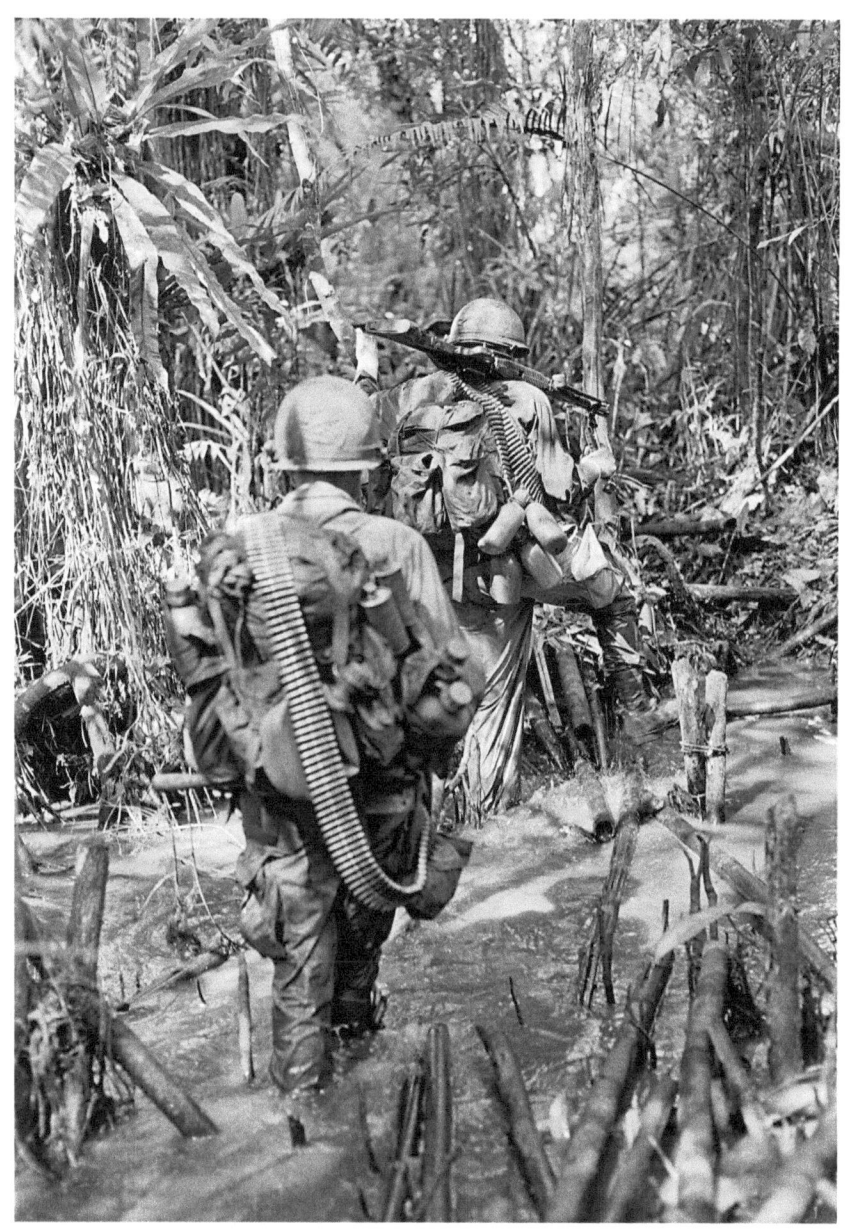

The Cambodian invasion had ended in June of 1970, eliminating vast quantities of Communist men and material, and pushing NVA strongholds deeper into Cambodia. The ARVN had proved itself battle worthy, and now it was taking on a more prominent role in military operations. The slow transition in command was called the "Vietnamization program." From the viewpoint of a lot of grunts it was one more reason not to become a statistic. Nobody wanted to be the last American casualty. It was the beginning of the end of the war.

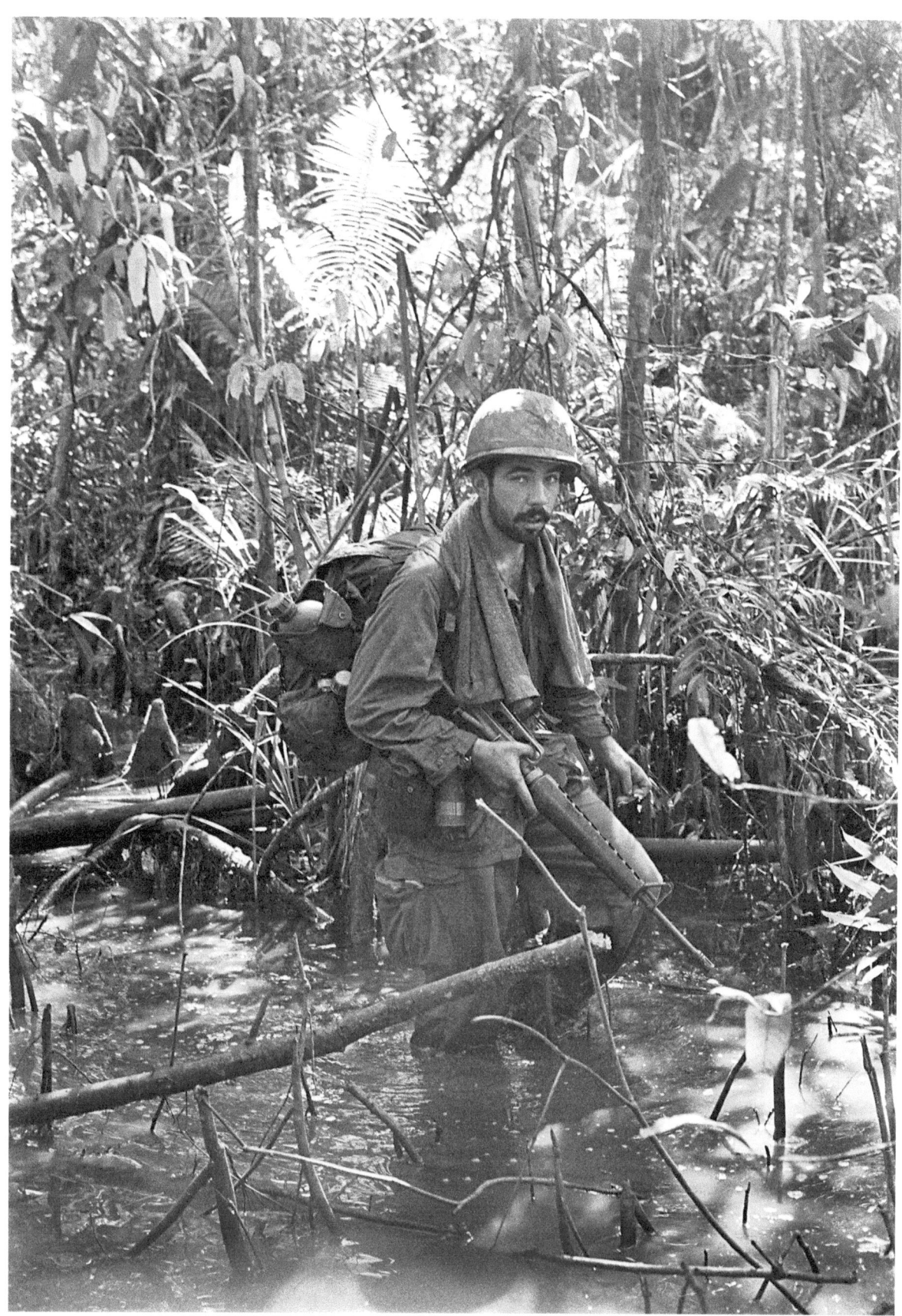

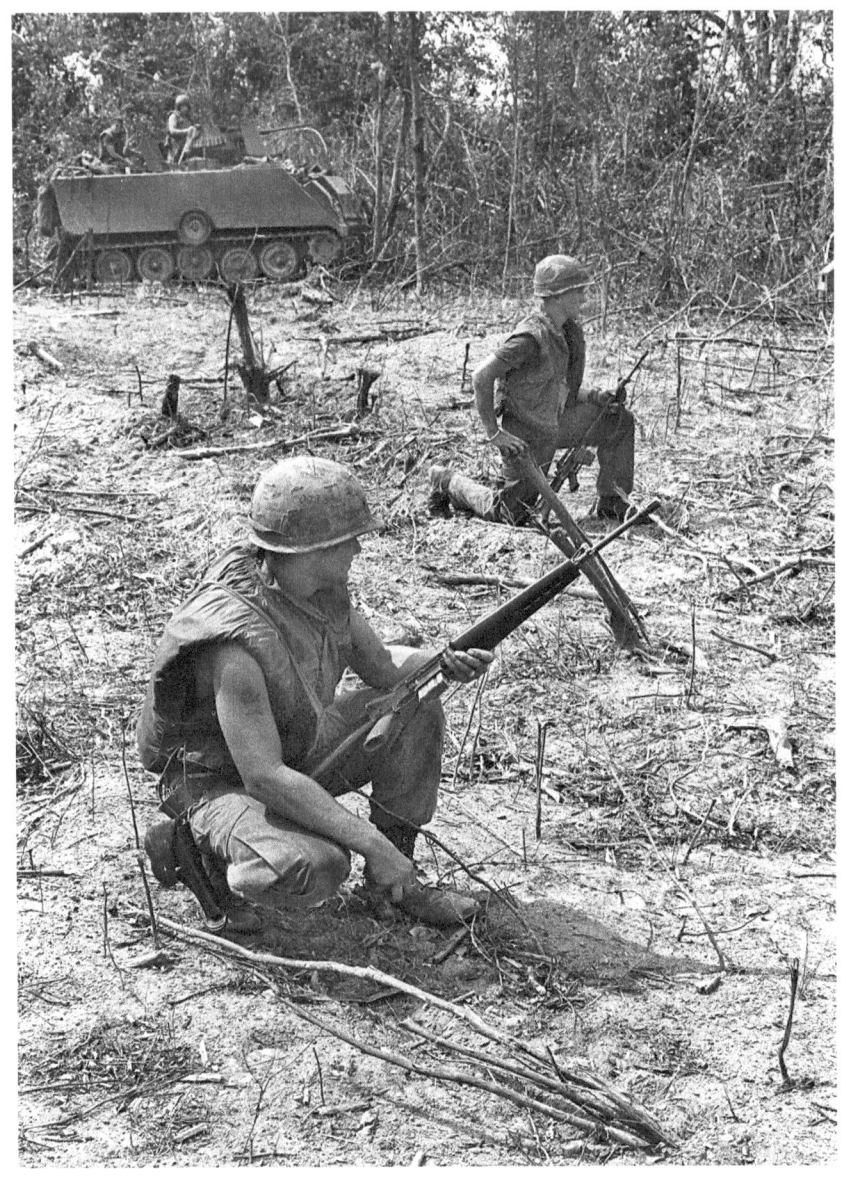

The 221st Signal Corps was based at Long Binh near Saigon, and that is where I began and ended every mission. Most of my assignments were in the delta region, although some job locations were farther north. Sometimes I traveled by myself, sometimes as part of a writer/motion picture/still photographer team. After several weeks in the field photographers returned to Long Binh to turn in film, write captions, and pick up orders for another assignment.

Assignments could be vague, like documenting whatever the 25th Infantry happened to be doing in some given location, or more precise; photographing the Special forces recon school near Nha Trang.

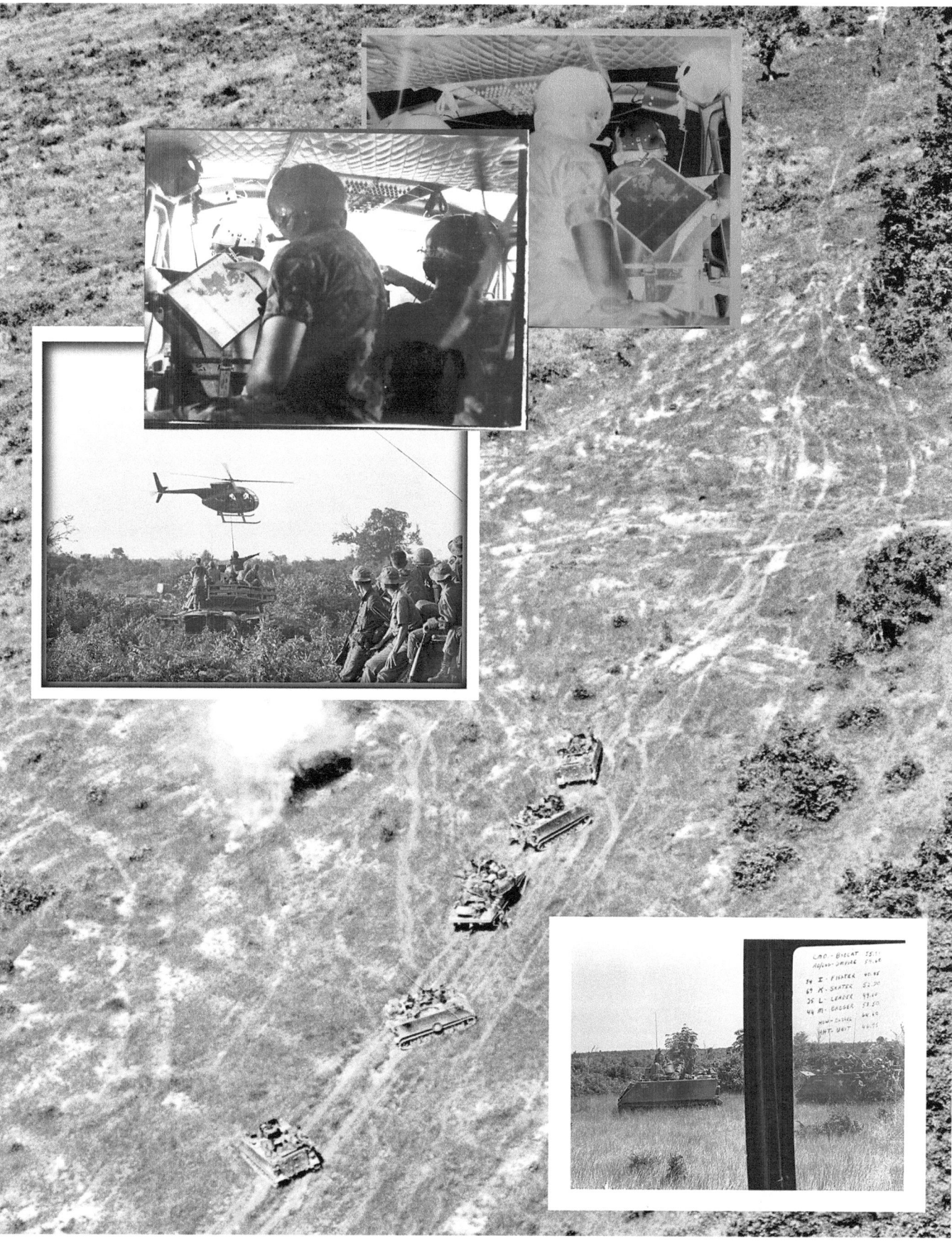

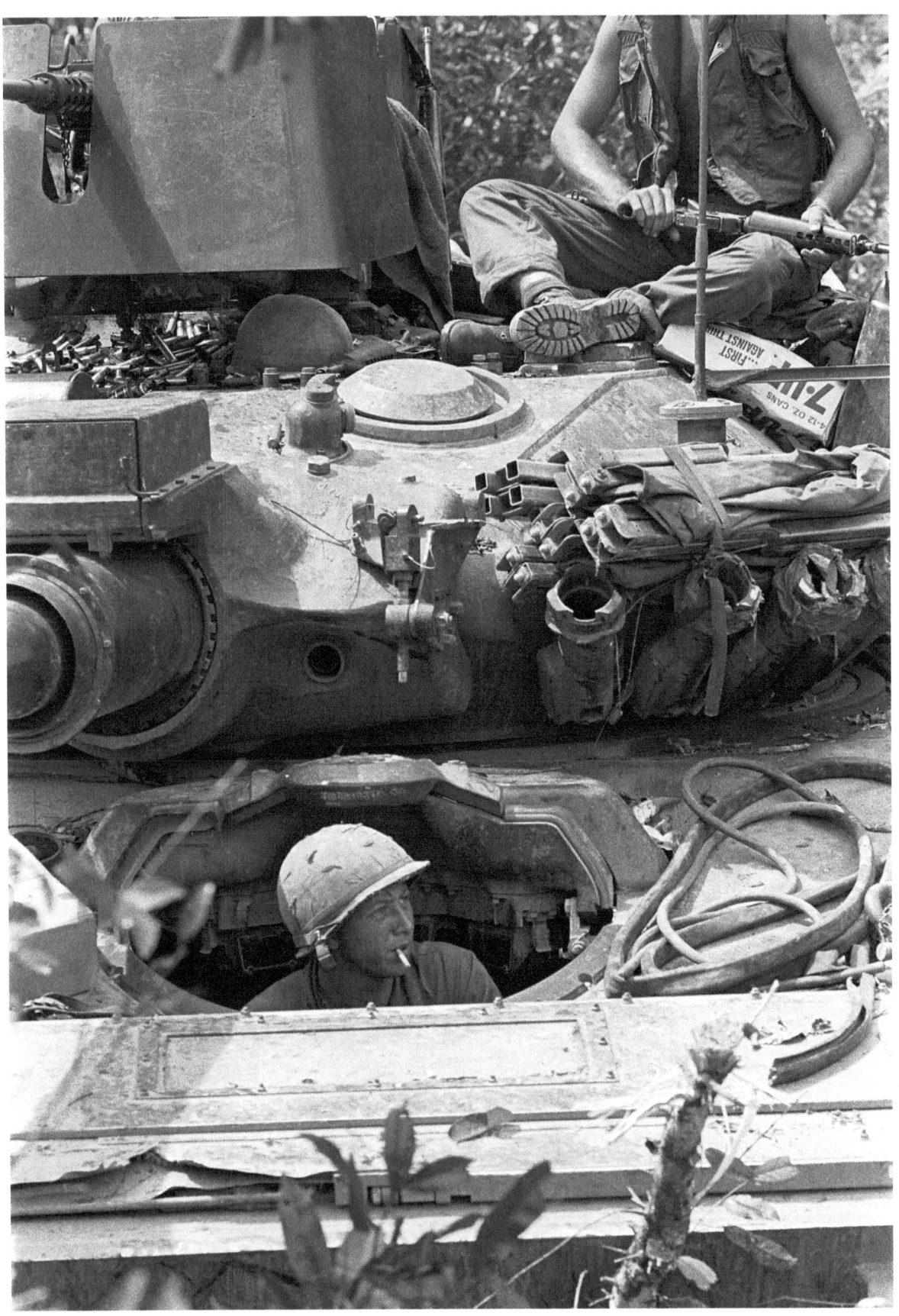

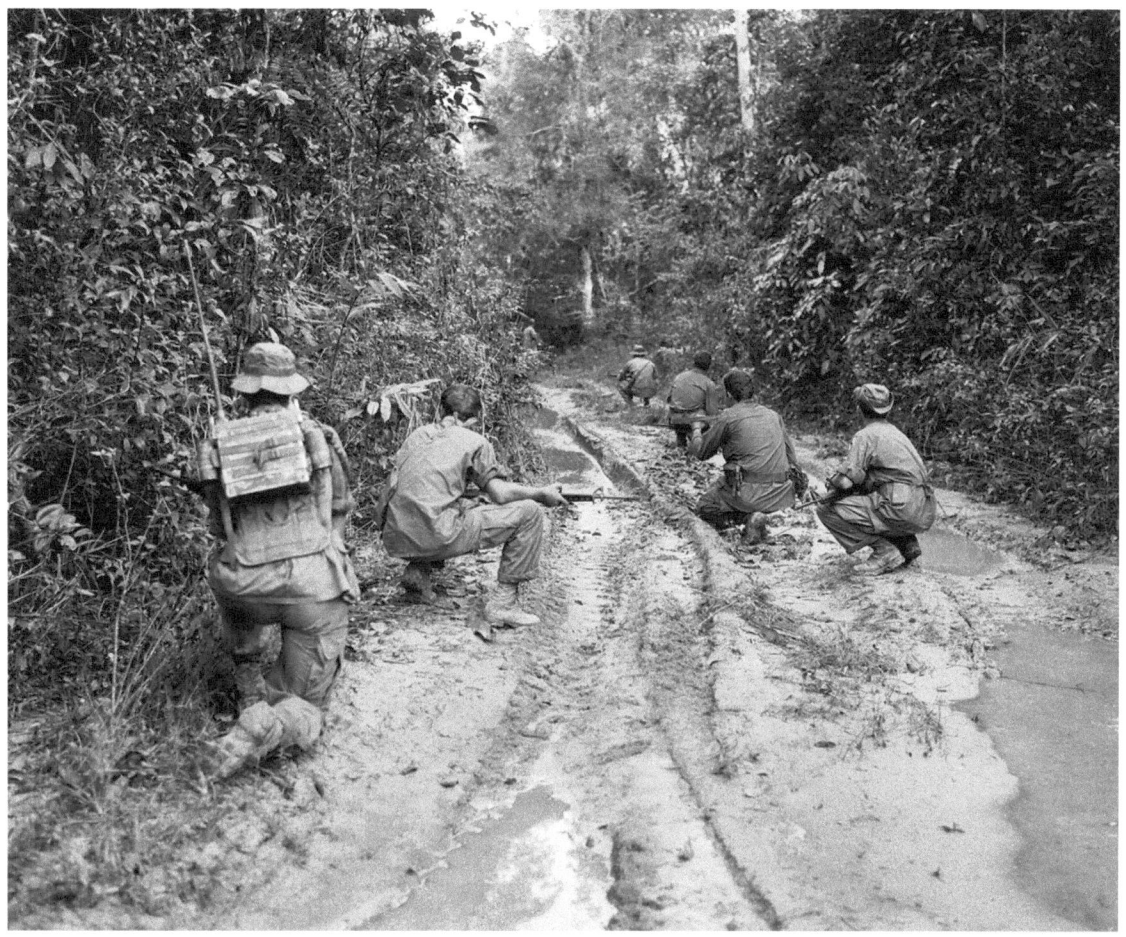

For logistical reasons the military divided South Vietnam into four sections. I corps, (eye corps), was located next to the DMZ, the dividing line between North and South Vietnam. II and part of III corps were elevated enough to be considered central highlands. IV corps was low country, wedged between the South China Sea, the Gulf of Siam, and Cambodia. I saw all four sections but spent most of my time in III and IV corps with the 11th Armored Cavalry Regiment or their supporting infantry units. The 11th ACRs track vehicles were ideal for transporting troops through light brush, but less effective in jungle and marshy soil.

In the dry season, the tracks churned the dirt into a fine powder that settled in every crack and crevice. Weapons and camera gear needed constant attention, but that was a small price to pay for the transportation and firepower.

In "bush country" the massive vehicles leveled small trees and cleared paths through otherwise hard to negotiate terrain. The smell of diesel exhaust and churned earth was always present, and riding in a column of tanks induced a feeling of power that was strong during daylight, but dissipated in the evening.

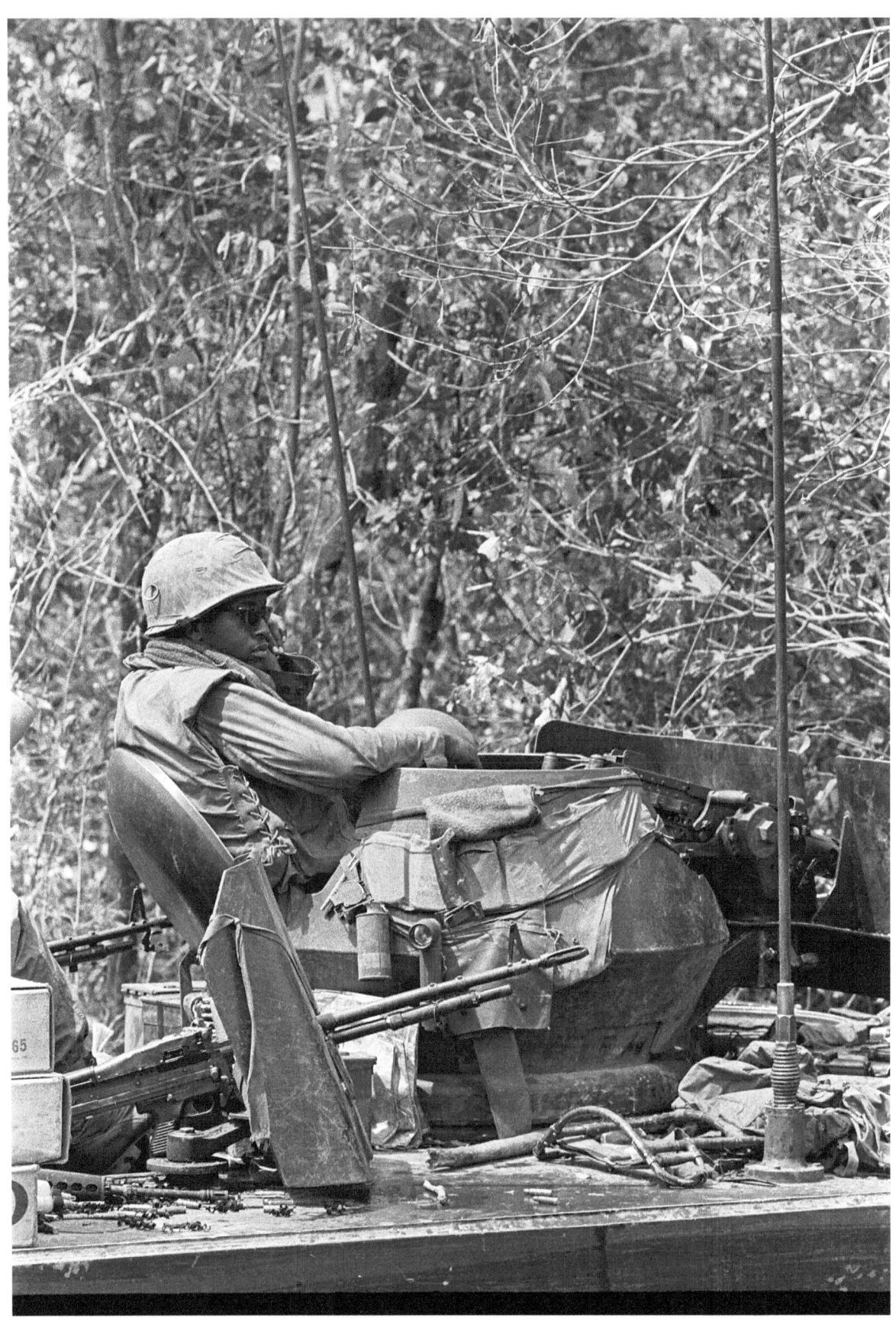

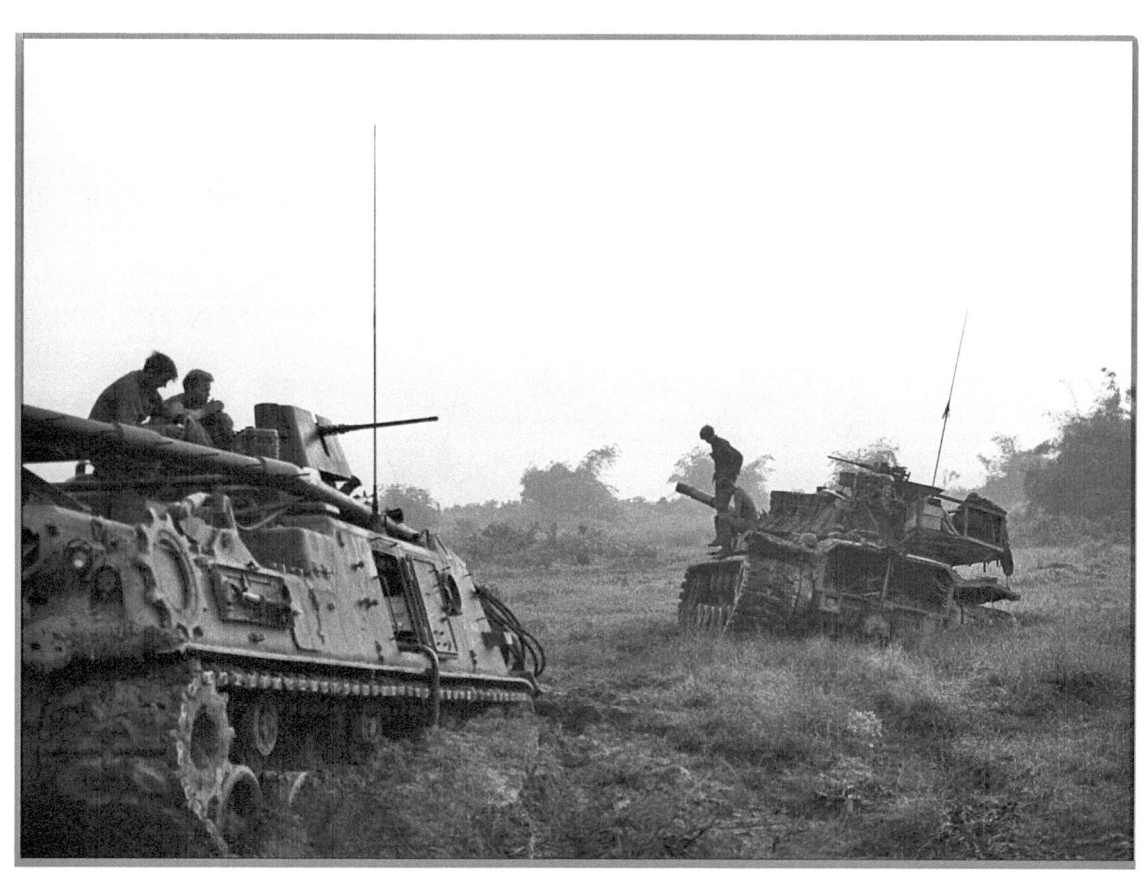

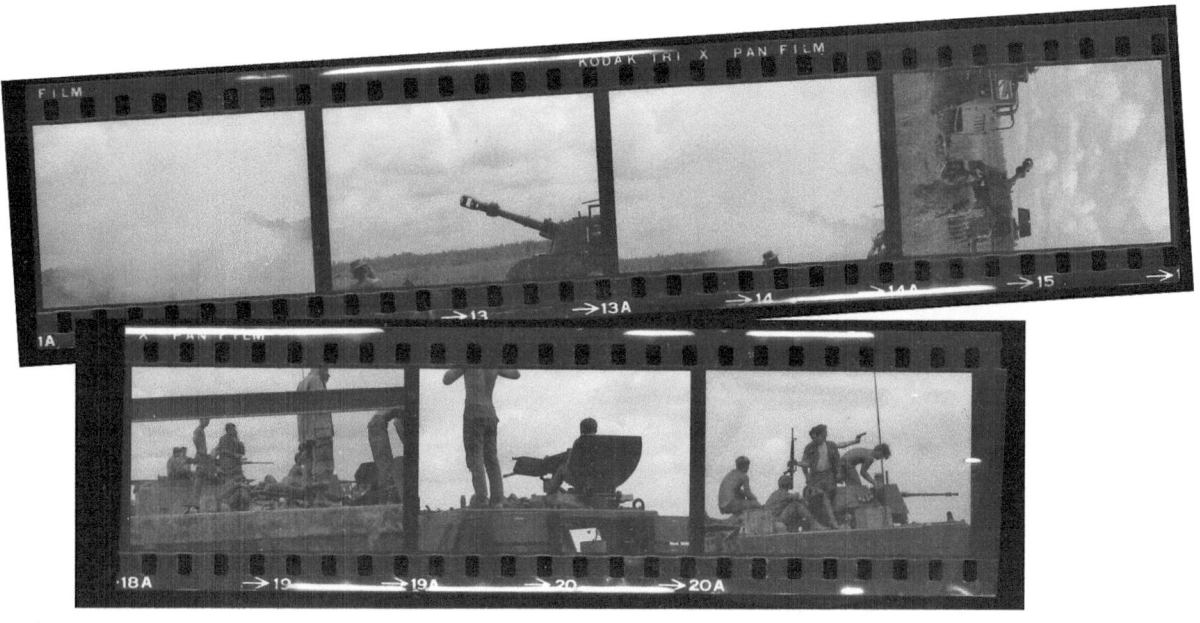

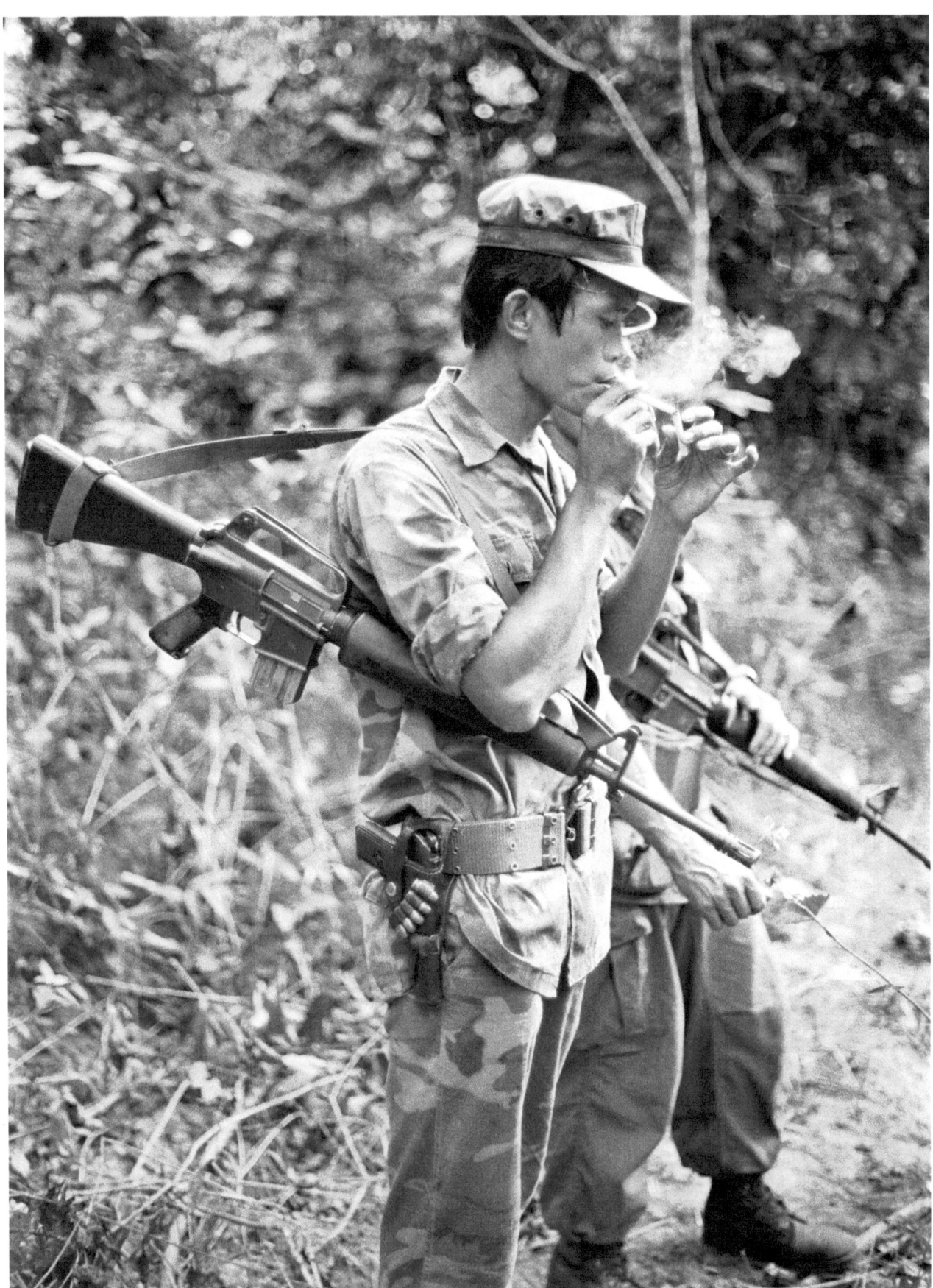

Sections of jungle were littered with propaganda. This leaflet depicts a North Vietnamese Army soldier being repatriated. Our side dropped them in strategic areas around Vietnam as part of the Chieu Hoi, (open arms), program that was instituted in the mid-60s. It was an amnesty offer to the enemy for swapping sides, and the program was having some success. The defectors were generally referred to as Hoi Chan, meaning they transferred allegiance under the "open arms" program.

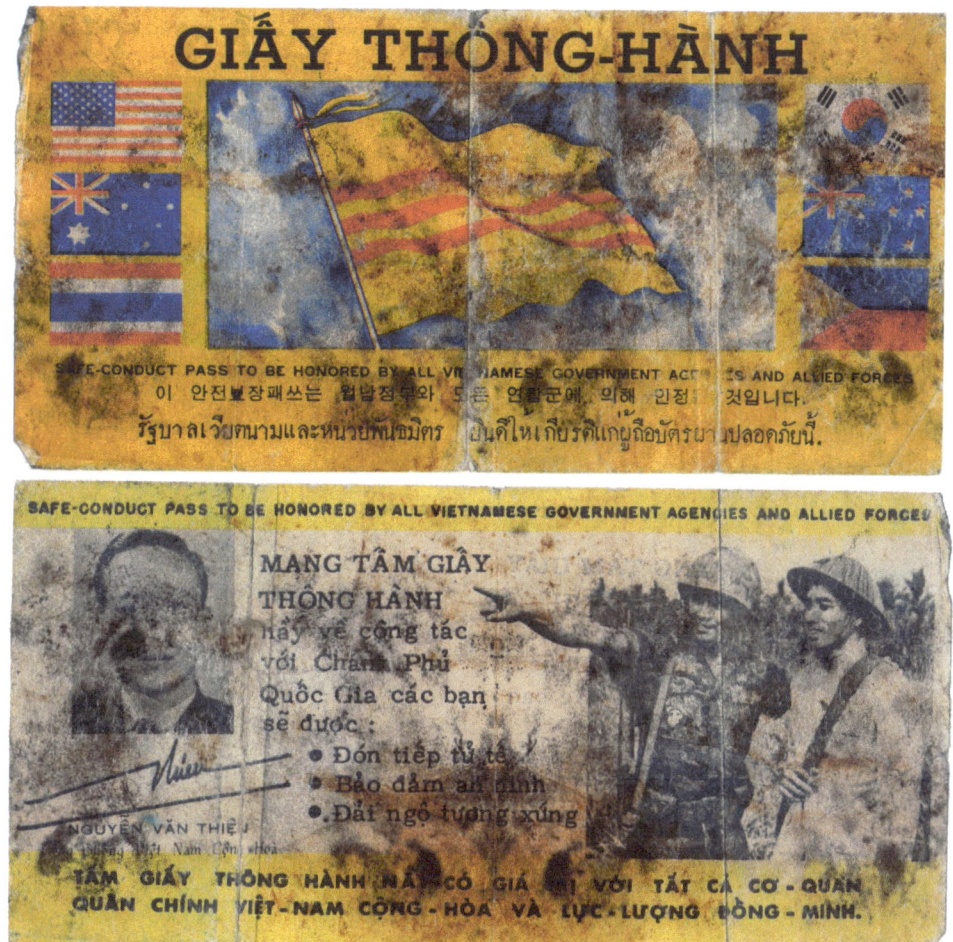

The soldier on the opposite page was a scout for the 11th ACR and seemed to have gained the confidence of the US troops he traveled with. He was very animated, and once demonstrated with his machete how he liked to sever the heads of Viet Cong. Defectors like him that traveled with US troops were referred to as Kit Carson scouts.

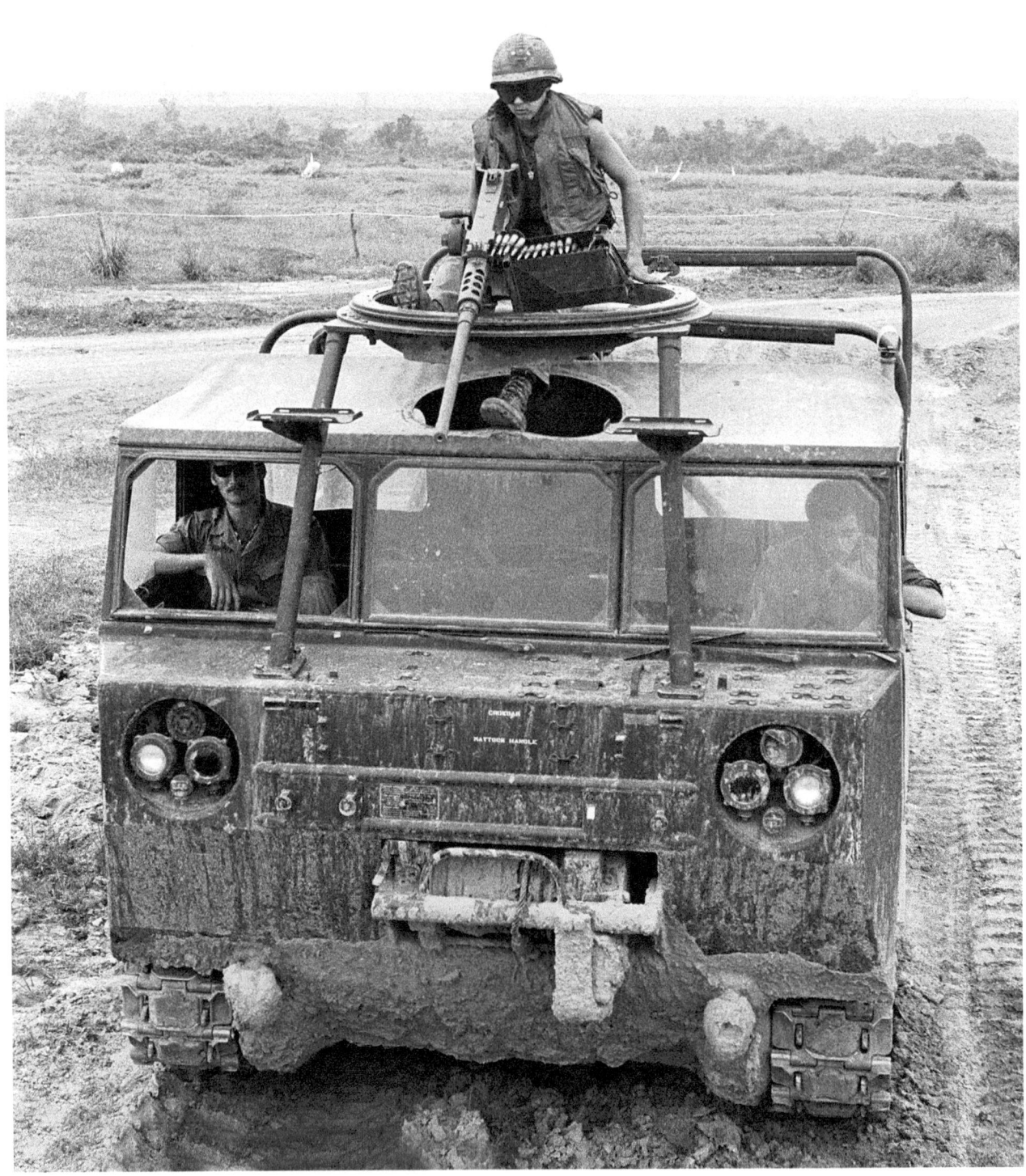

There are advanced military schools that teach combat photography. I suspect part of the training deals with conduct and protocol in a combat zone. They probably teach things like "never get between a M-60 gunner and the grunts that carry his ammo belts." I missed that course and all the other ones too, but decided not to mention it to the press Corp Sergeant. It would be too easy for the PIO to exchange my camera for a rifle and send me off to a line unit. Instead, I kept a low profile and monitored myself constantly. The success of my first assignment provided a much needed confidence boost, and the magnitude of all that I did not know began to dissolve.

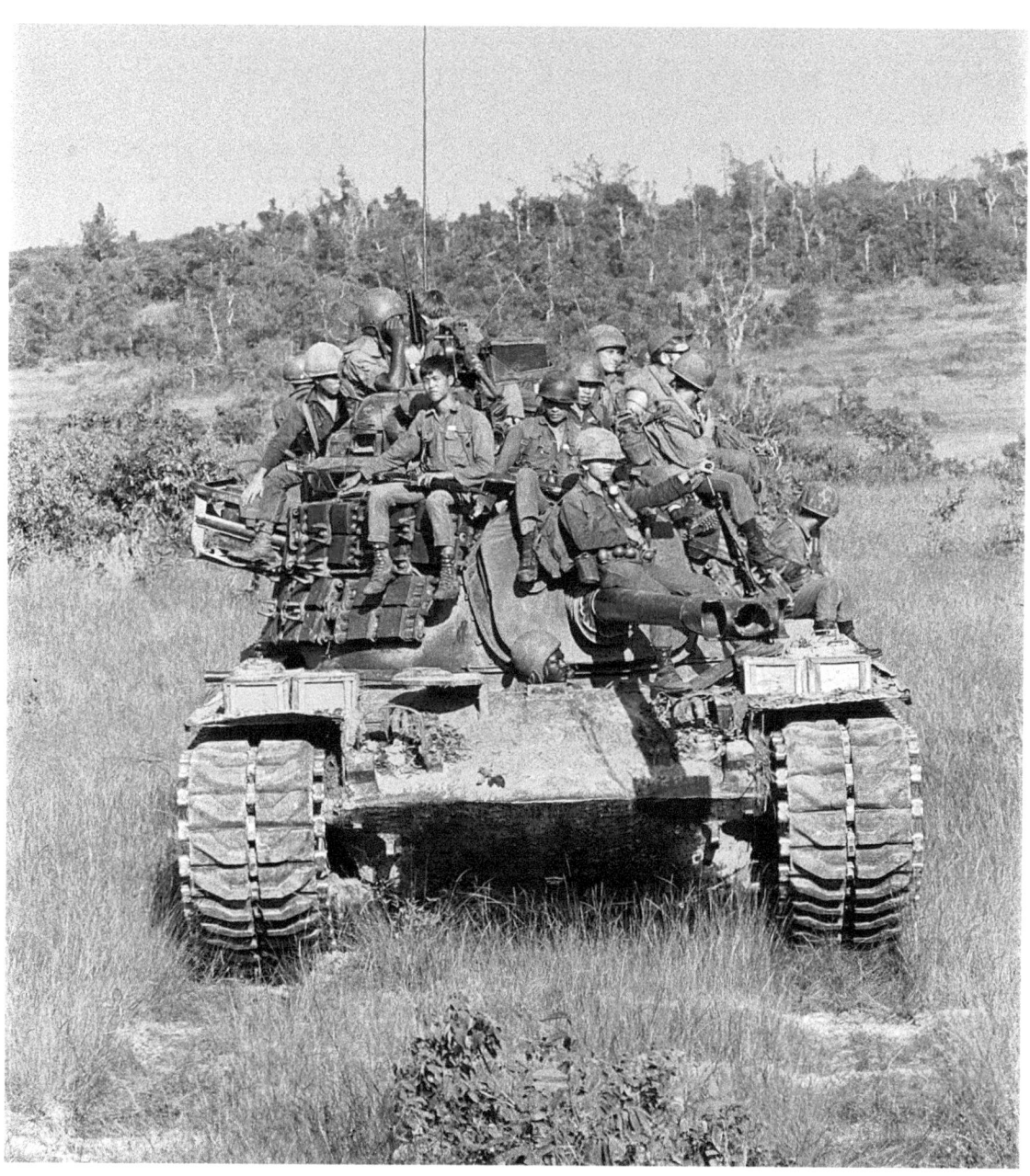

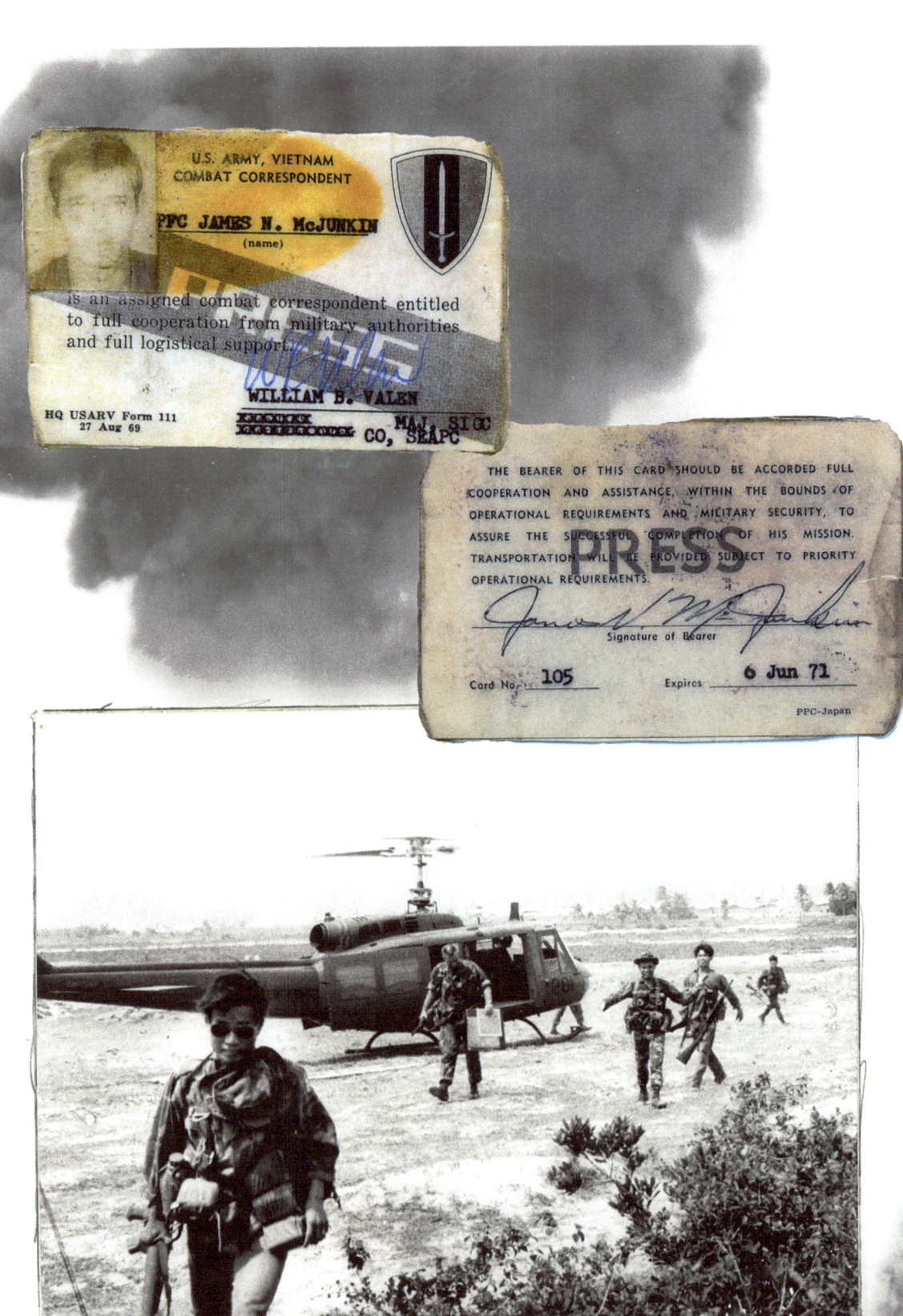

U.S. ARMY, VIETNAM
COMBAT CORRESPONDENT

PFC JAMES N. McJUNKIN
(name)

is an assigned combat correspondent entitled
to full cooperation from military authorities
and full logistical support.

WILLIAM B. VALEN

HQ USARV Form 111
27 Aug 69
                                    MAJ, SIGC
                              CO, SEAPC

THE BEARER OF THIS CARD SHOULD BE ACCORDED FULL
COOPERATION AND ASSISTANCE, WITHIN THE BOUNDS OF
OPERATIONAL REQUIREMENTS AND MILITARY SECURITY, TO
ASSURE THE SUCCESSFUL COMPLETION OF HIS MISSION.
TRANSPORTATION WILL BE PROVIDED SUBJECT TO PRIORITY
OPERATIONAL REQUIREMENTS.

PRESS

Signature of Bearer

Card No. 105   Expires   6 Jun 71

PPC-Japan

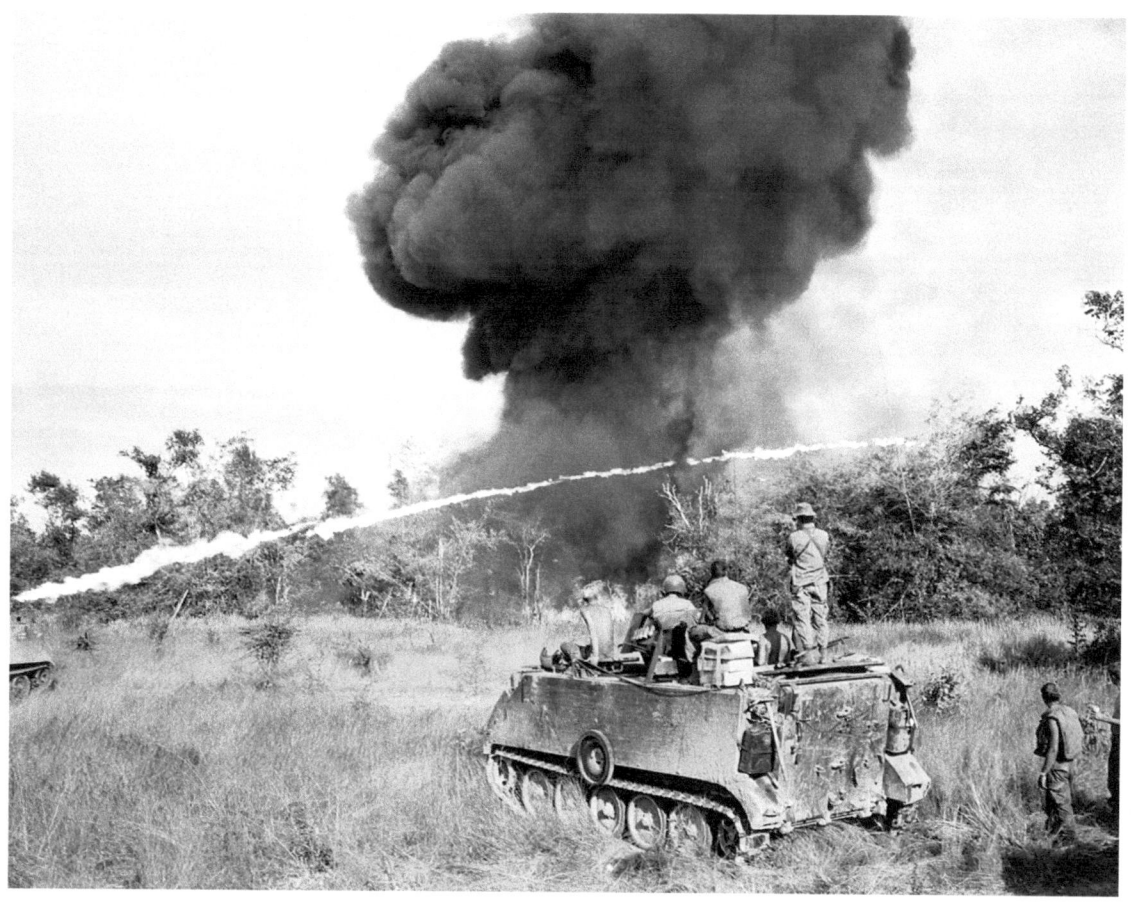

In addition to travel orders, Army correspondents carried a press card that helped navigate the way through military bureaucracy. The front of the card had the name and picture of the correspondent. My card stated that PFC James N. McJunkin is an assigned combat correspondent entitled to full cooperation from military authorities and full logistical support. The card was usually all that was necessary to catch a ride on the next available chopper or Air America plane headed towards my destination. It added weight to my rank and I used it like a backstage pass.

I seldom traveled with the same correspondents, and I was never anywhere long enough to establish a real friendship. That bothered me less than the fact that in the bush I was always the FNG, (fucking new guy). In the bush I was with soldiers who lived and worked together and more or less knew what to expect from one another in any given situation. To them I was an unknown entity; the one who could be less than reliable. By the time I became trustworthy it was usually time to leave.

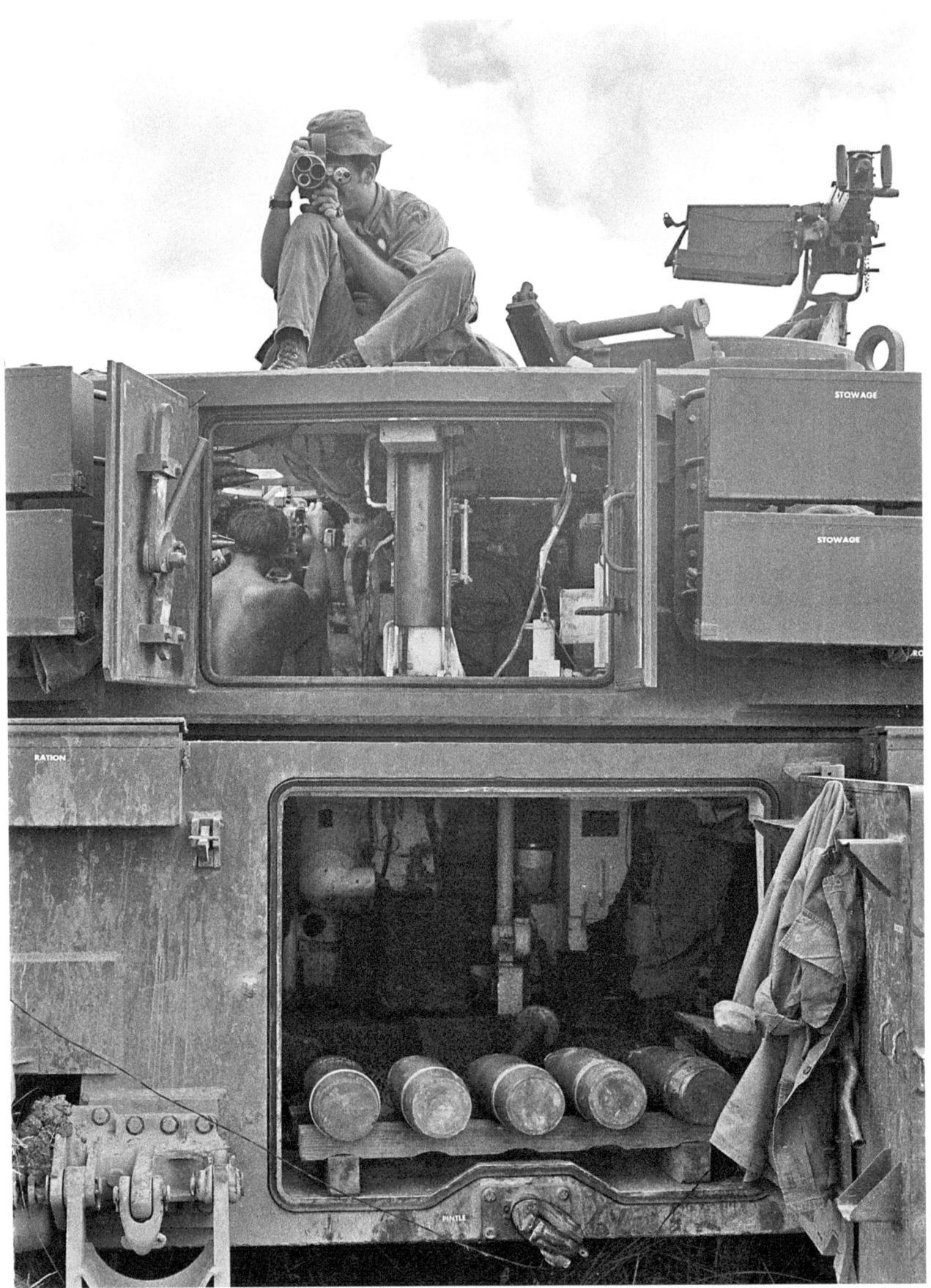

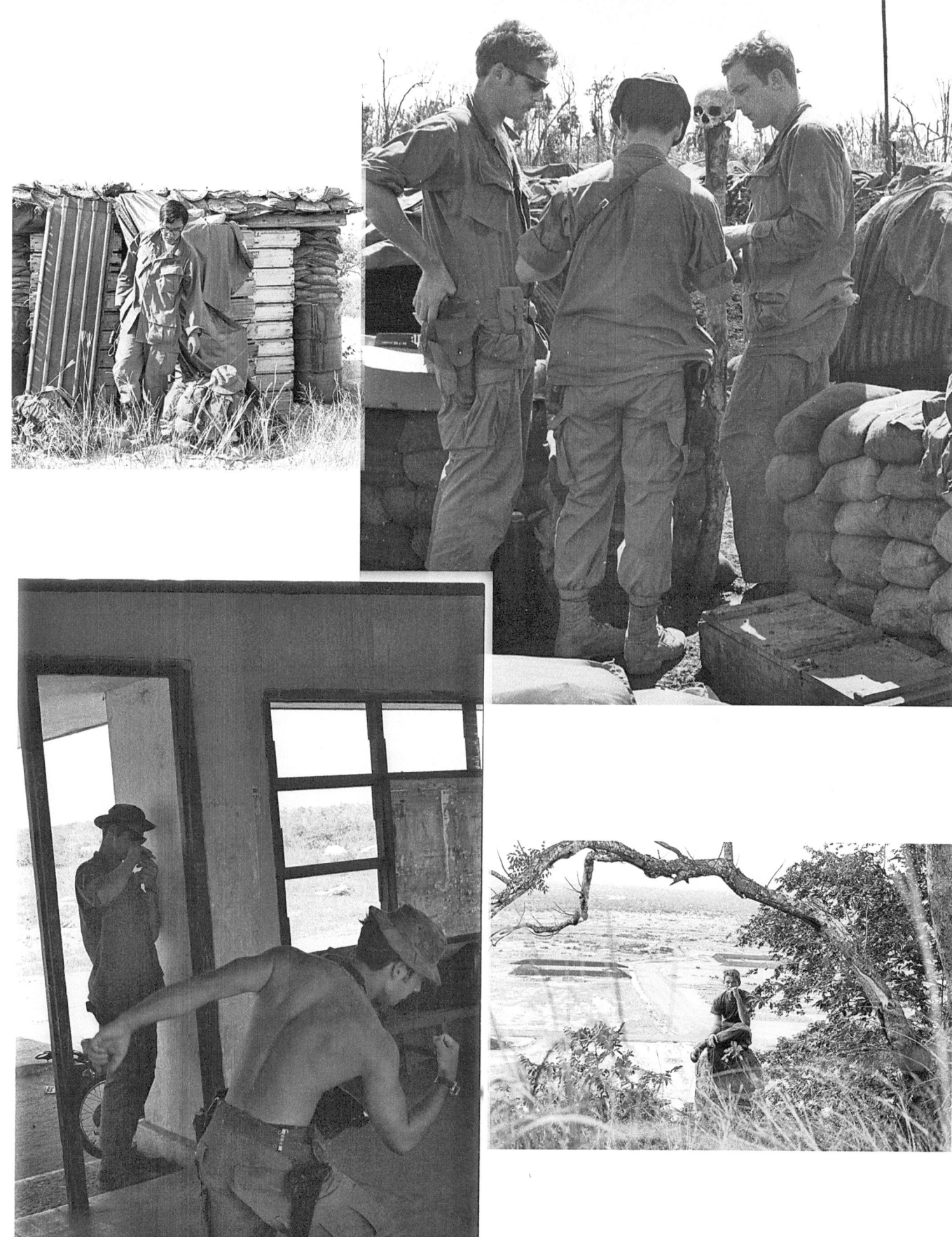

In November 1970 I flew to Nha Trang with a writer and a motion picture photographer for a story on the Special Forces RECON school. The school trained LRRPs (long range reconnaissance patrol) members and was a working base for RECON teams.

The teams consisted of four or five men who were inserted into a portion of jungle with just enough supplies and ammunition to complete their objective. Alone and outnumbered, their job was to observe rather than engage the enemy. Their longevity depended on stealth. Therefore, our access was restricted to a training mission on Hon Tre Island just off the coast of Vietnam, and to certain exercises at the school.

The Hon Tre Island excursion was uneventful. The helicopter ride over water was refreshingly cool and leaving the Vietnamese mainland seemed like wartime intermission.

One course objective was learning to rappel. The school had several tall platform towers that were used to simulate helicopter insertions in areas that the choppers were unable to land. All the students I saw mastered the rappelling techniques with ease, but the course objective was learning to rappel in full combat gear.

When walking, weight is easier to carry when it rides high on the back. That is the position most soldiers adjust their rucksacks. Rappelling requires a more horizontal posture, and gravity causes the extra weight to flip downward. The first few times they tried it almost all the trainees in full gear came down inverted.

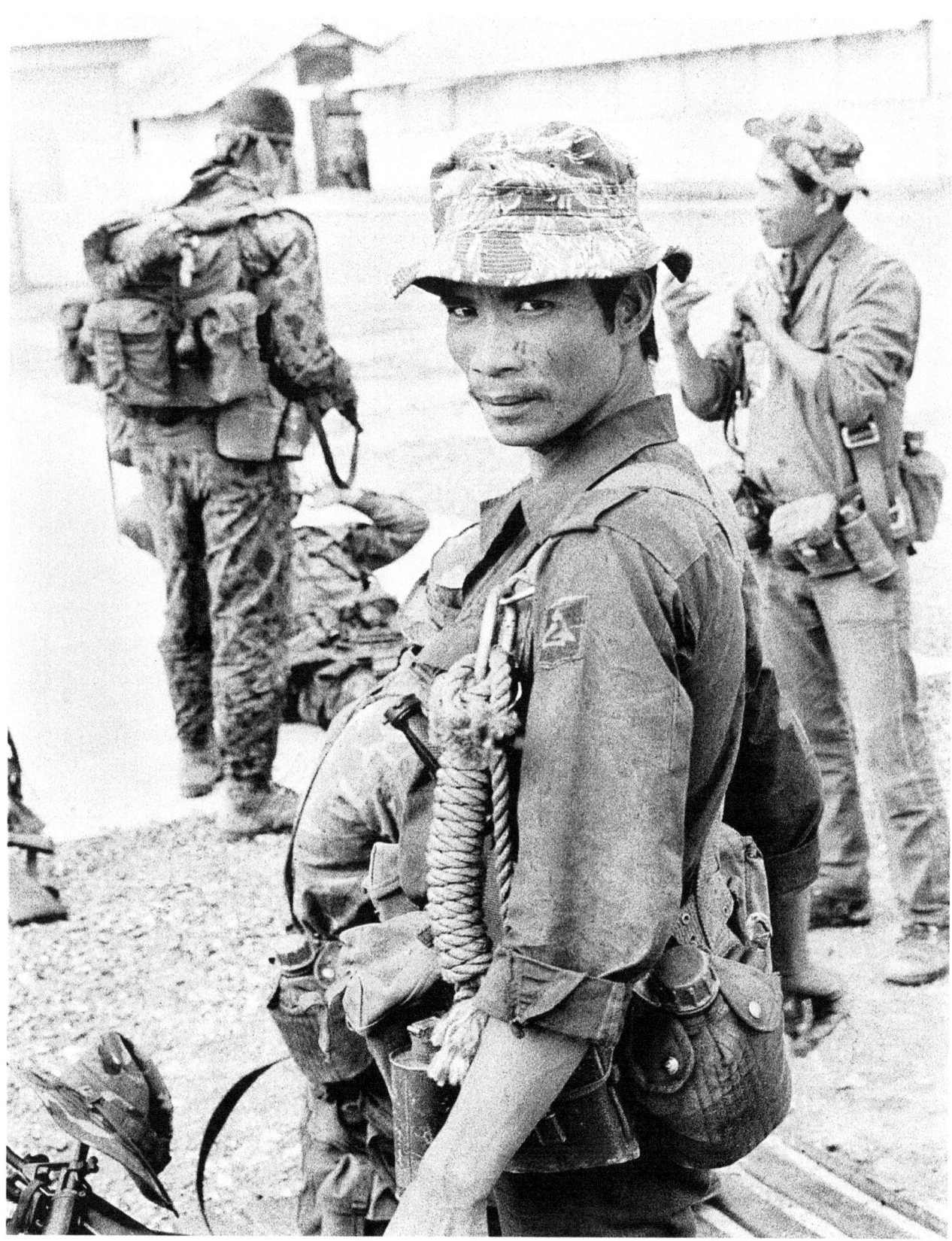

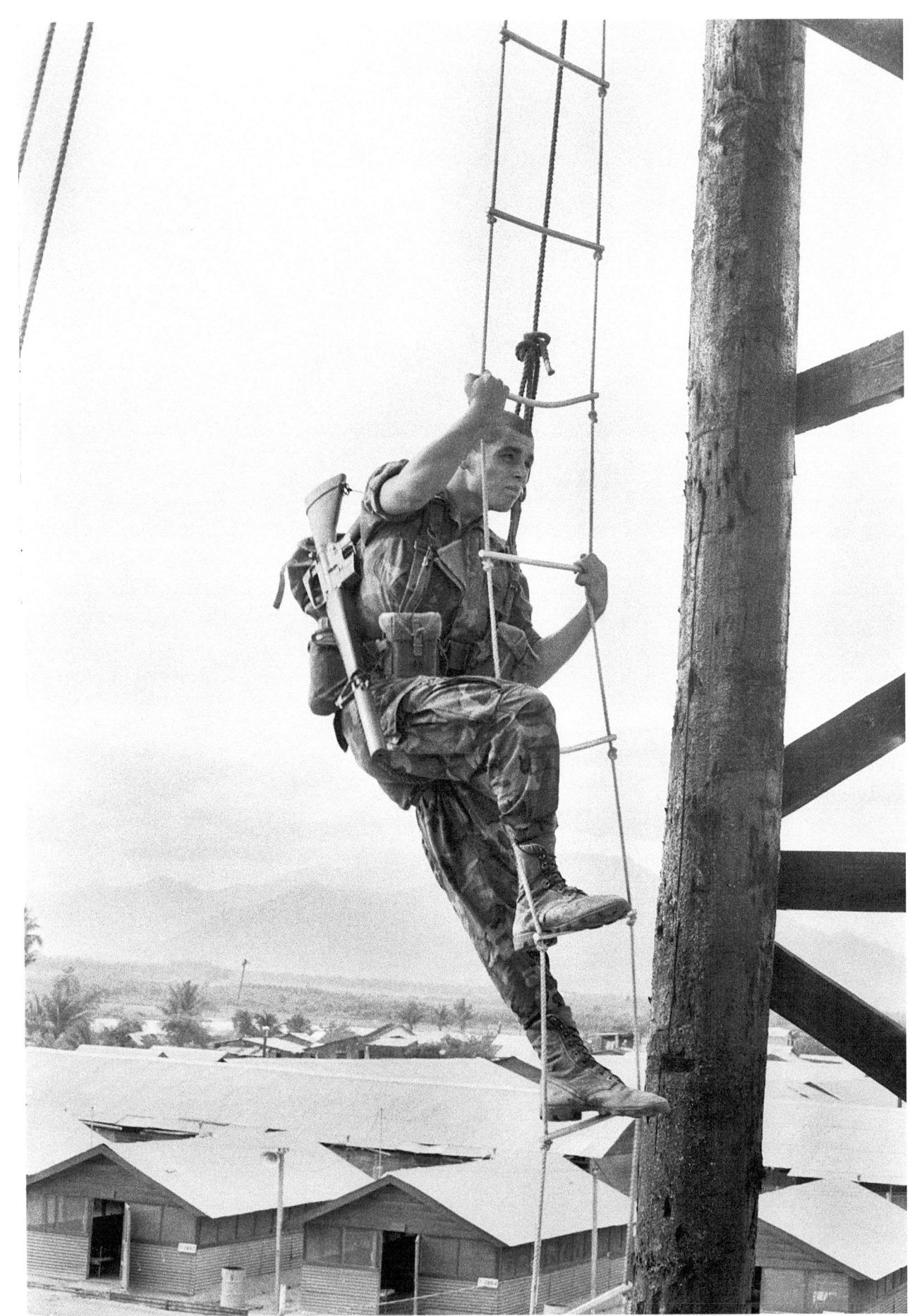

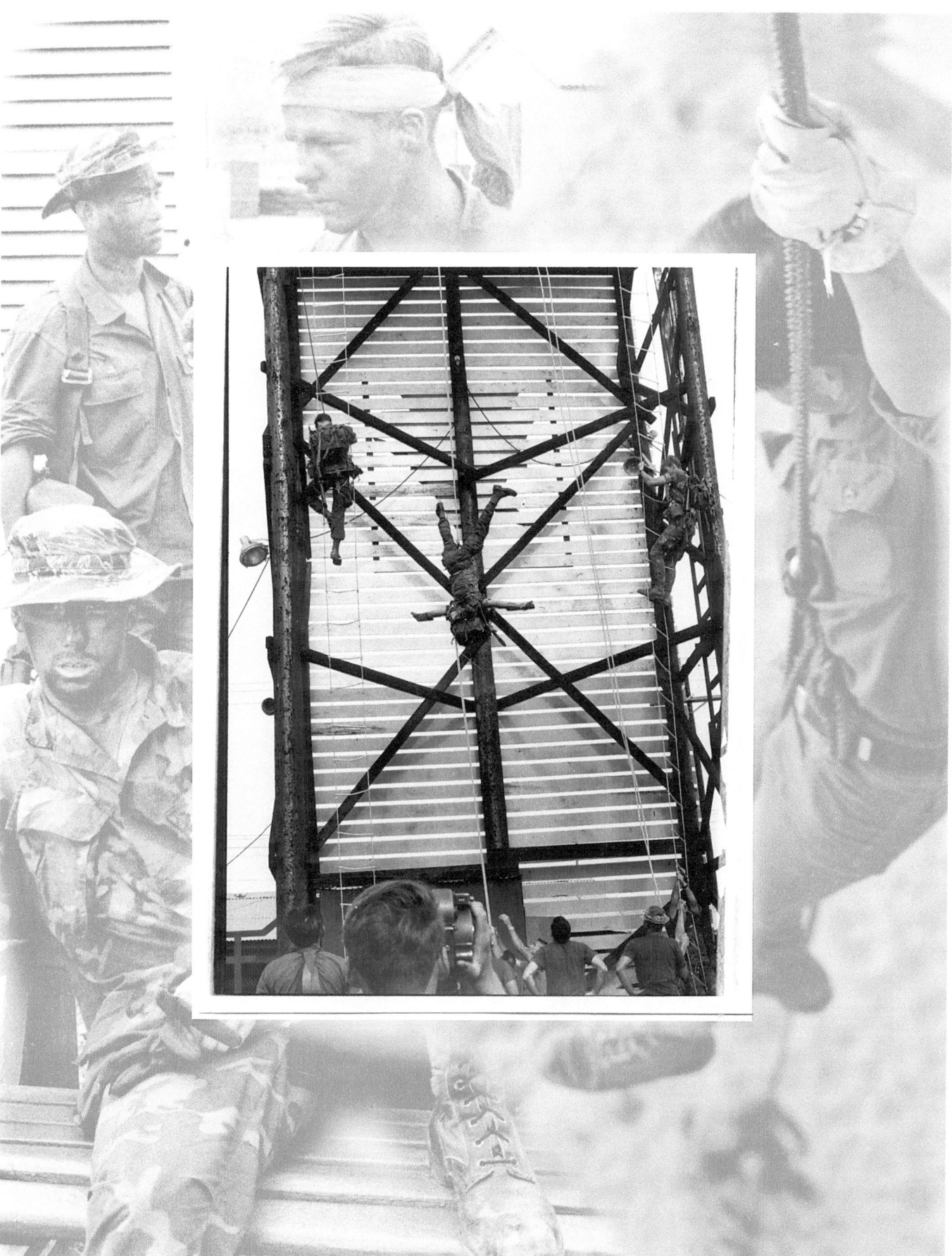

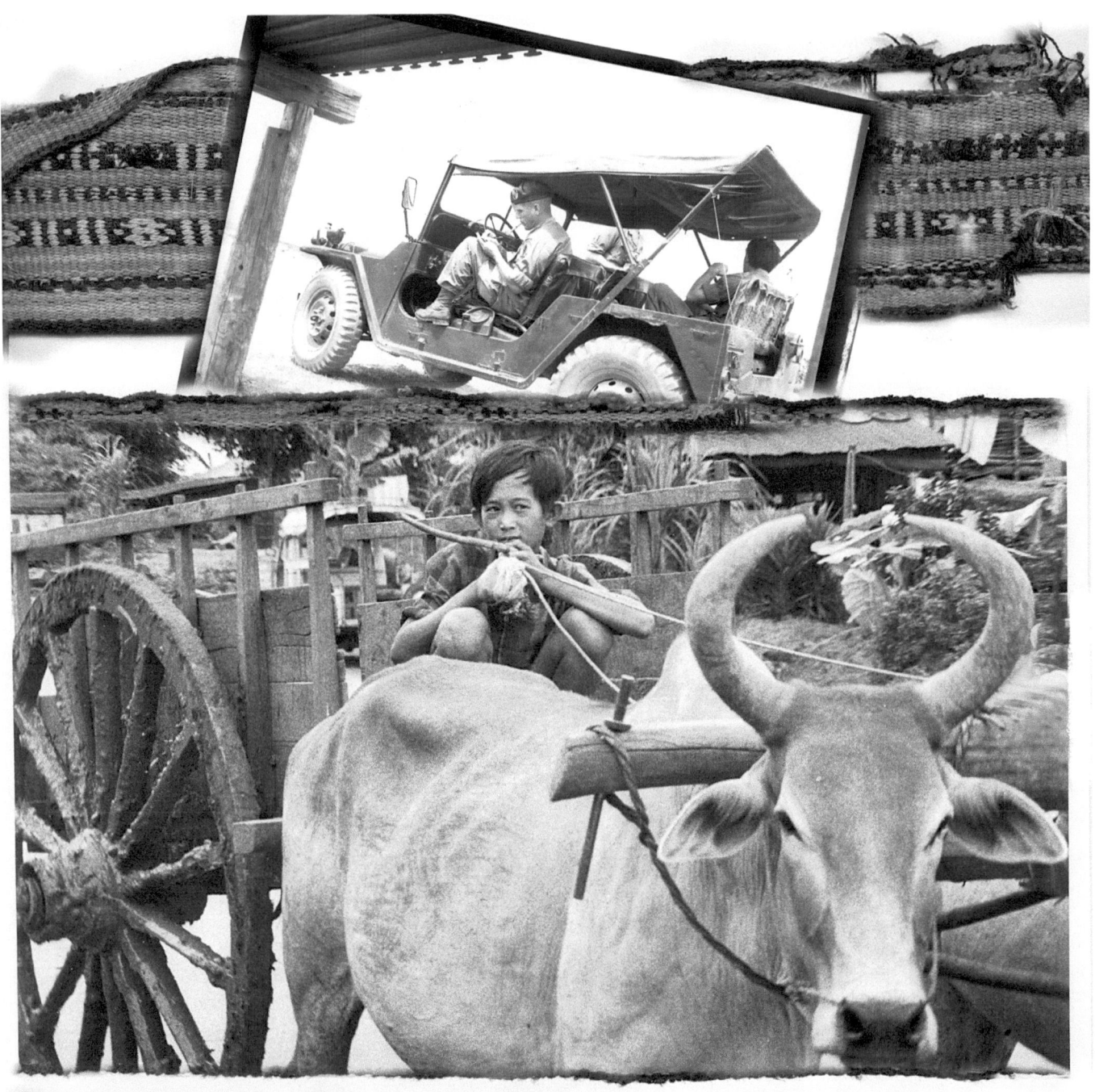

In the field I carried my personal 35mm camera as well as a variety of Army issue sizes and models. I shot my first assignment with a bulky 4x5-inch camera that might have been issued to me as a rite of initiation. Later, I traded the larger format for a 70mm Speed Grafflex, which was more suitable for the type of work I was doing.

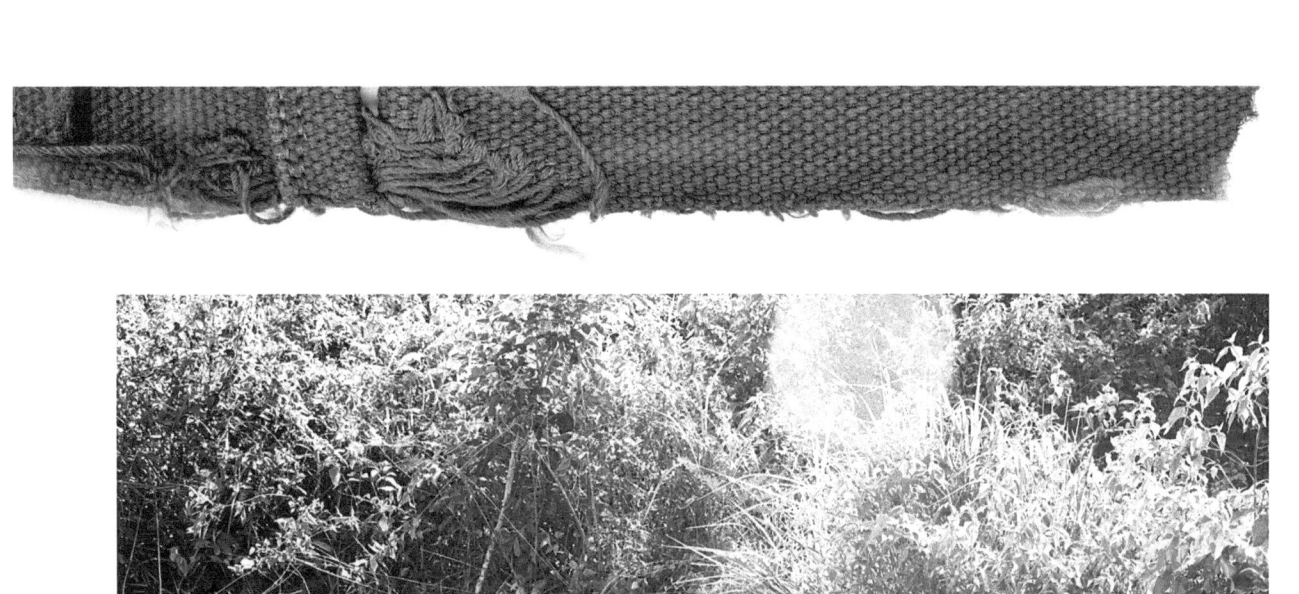

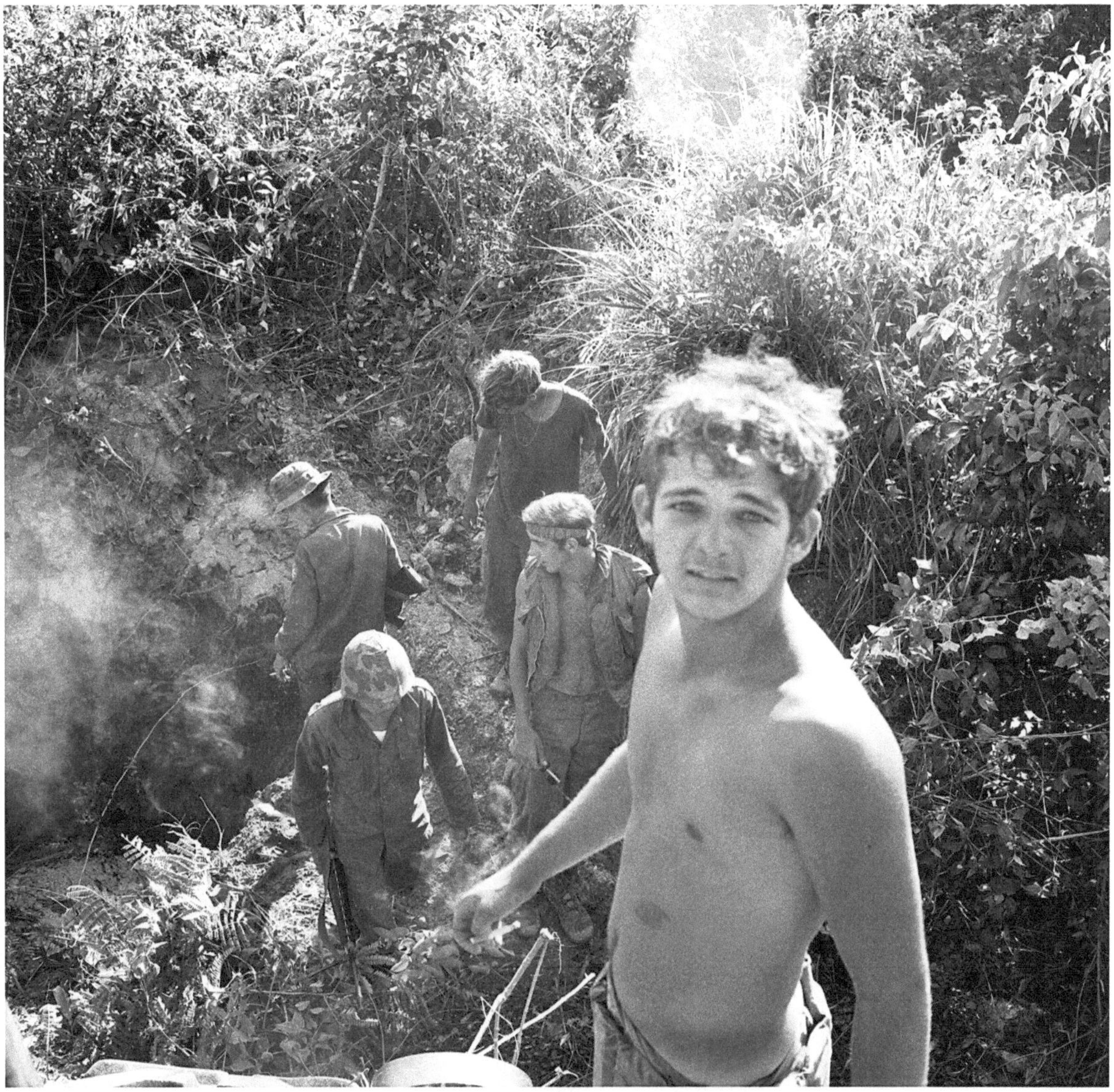

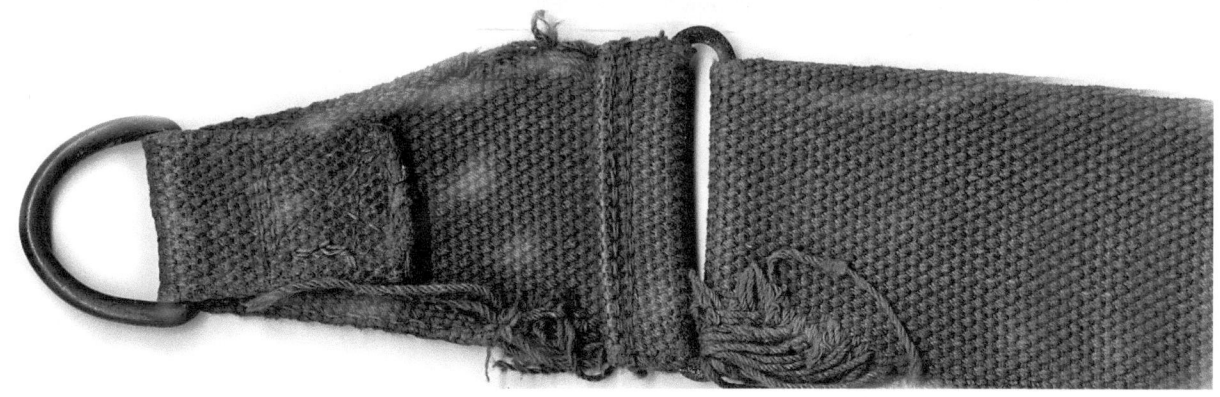

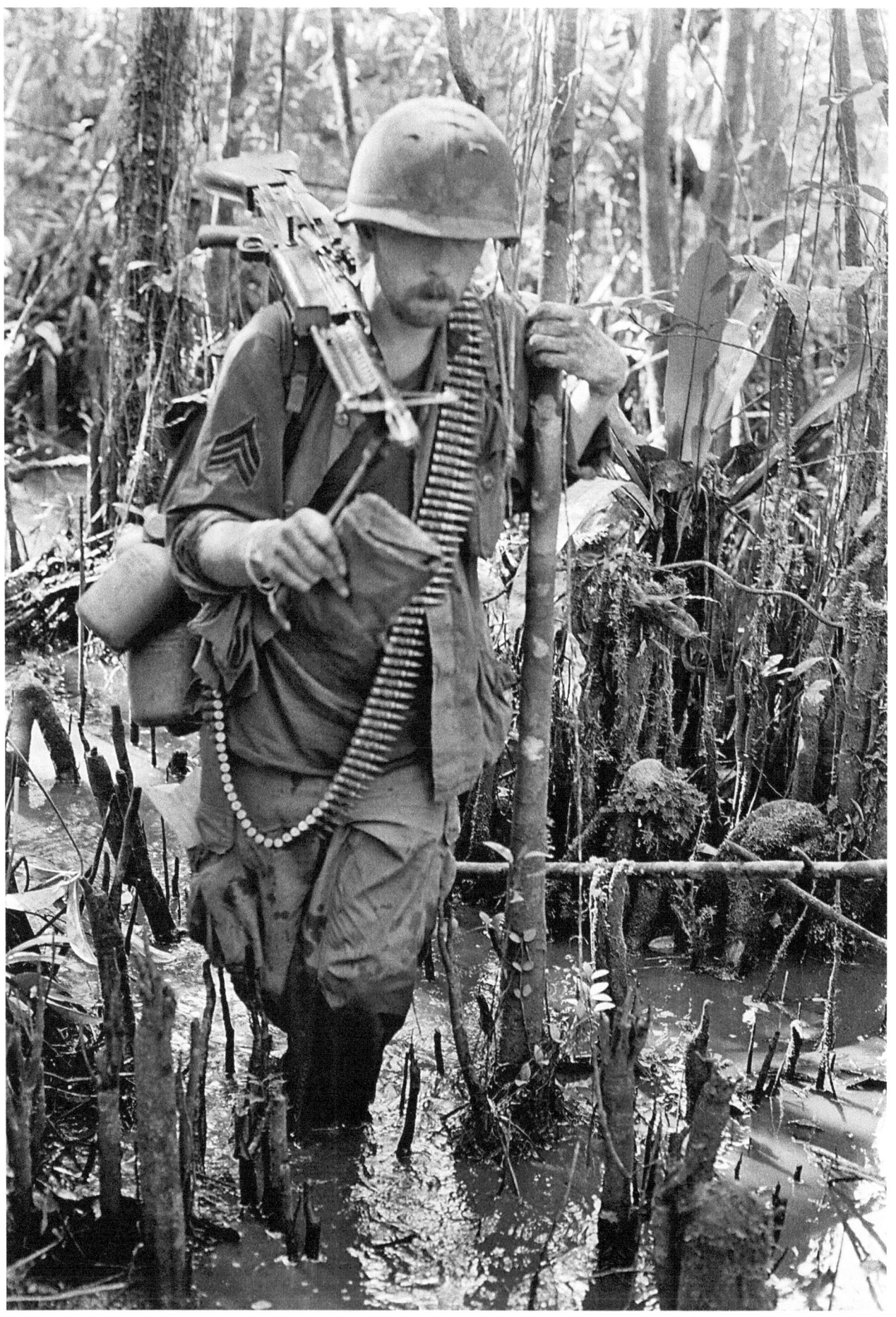

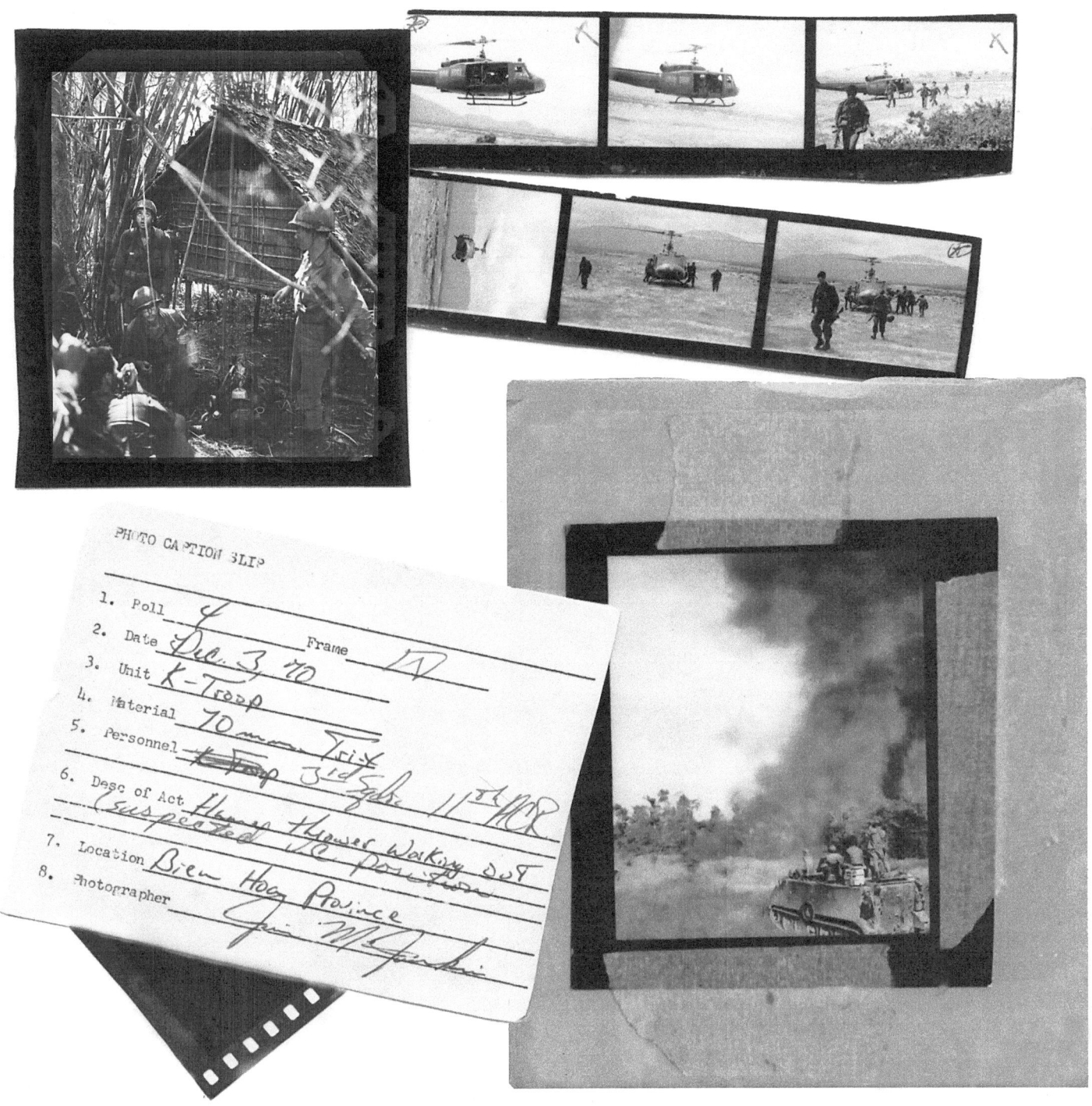

There is a way to calculate exposure settings according to film speed and daylight intensity and I eventually became mediocre at it. But in the jungle, where shafts of light penetrate the overhead canopy and everything else is in shadow, exposure settings were more confusing. Some of those exposures could have been better. Seeing the pictures became less of a problem than capturing the images.

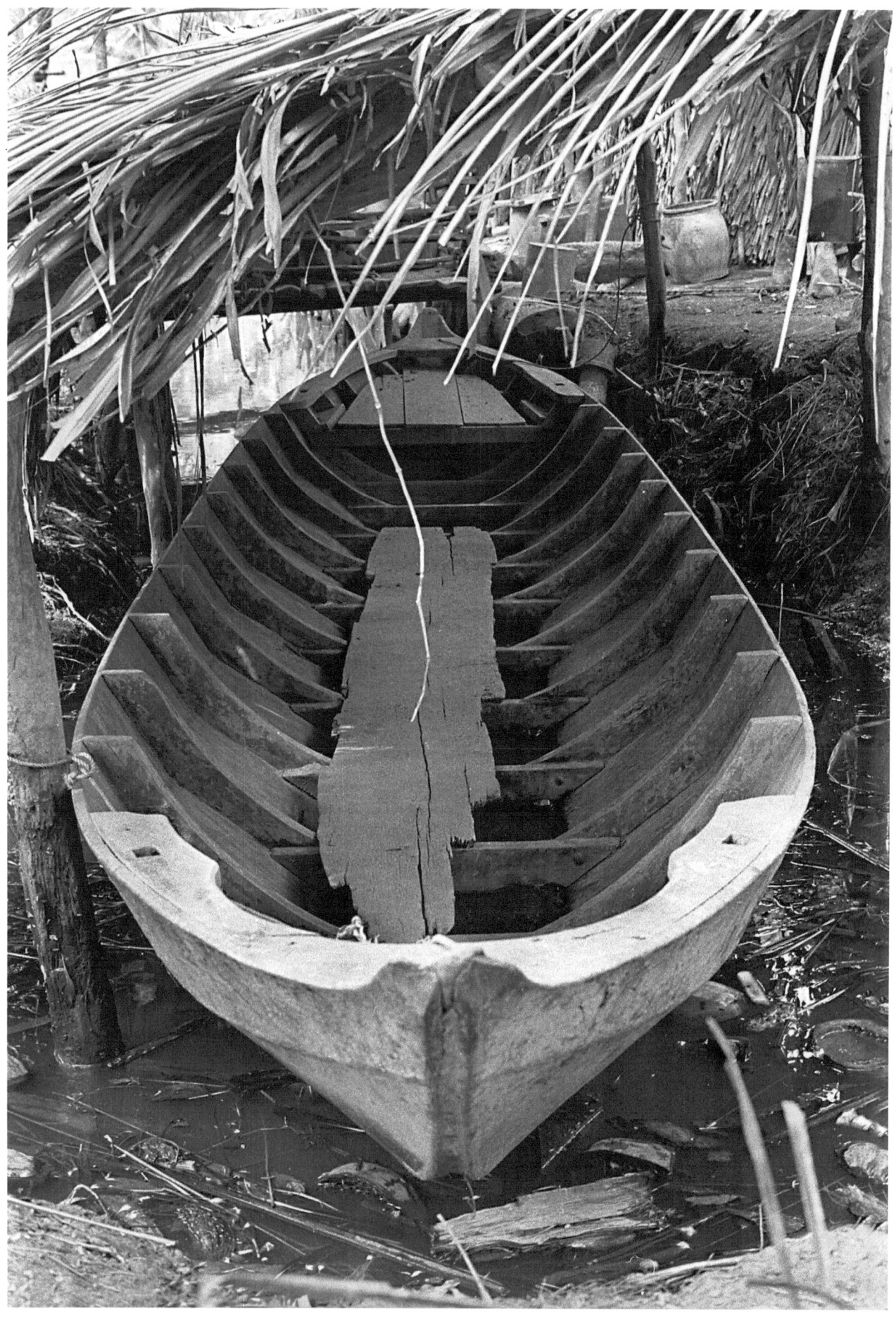

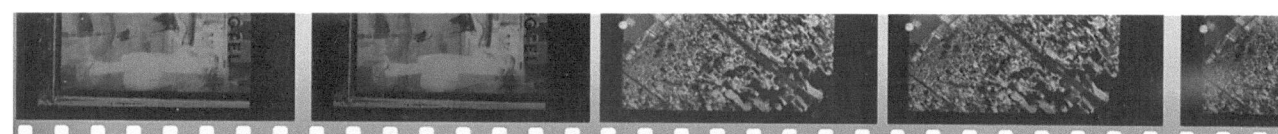

Still images tend to separate themselves from real time in an unfamiliar place, and Vietnam was beyond unfamiliar. It was strange enough to make the mundane exciting. Consequently, many of my pictures have nothing to do with military assignments.

My 35mm Nikkormat had an exposure meter that the 70mm was lacking. It allowed me to double check hard to guess settings and make some images for myself. The smaller format was so easy to carry and use that it began to take priority over my military camera.

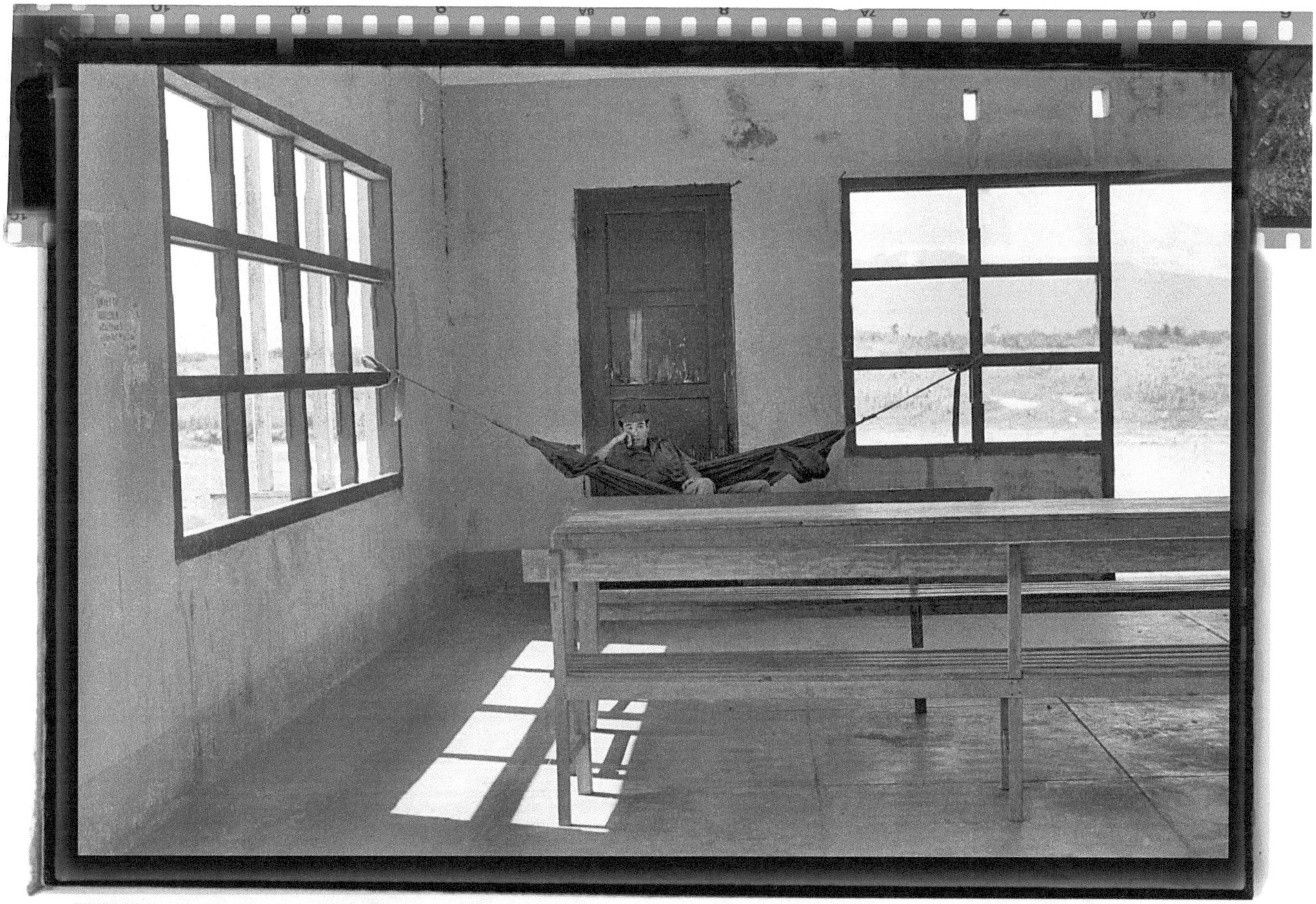

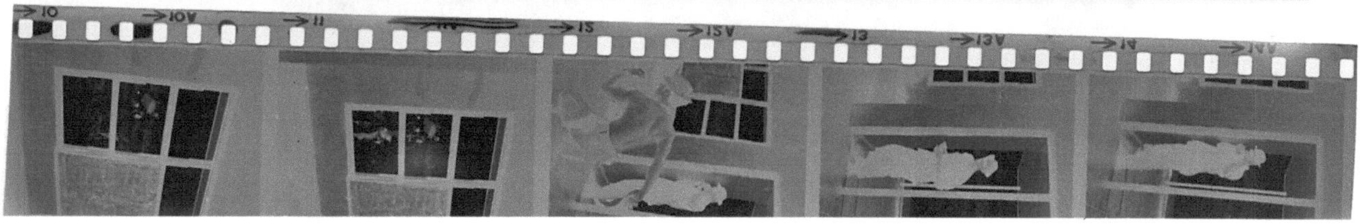

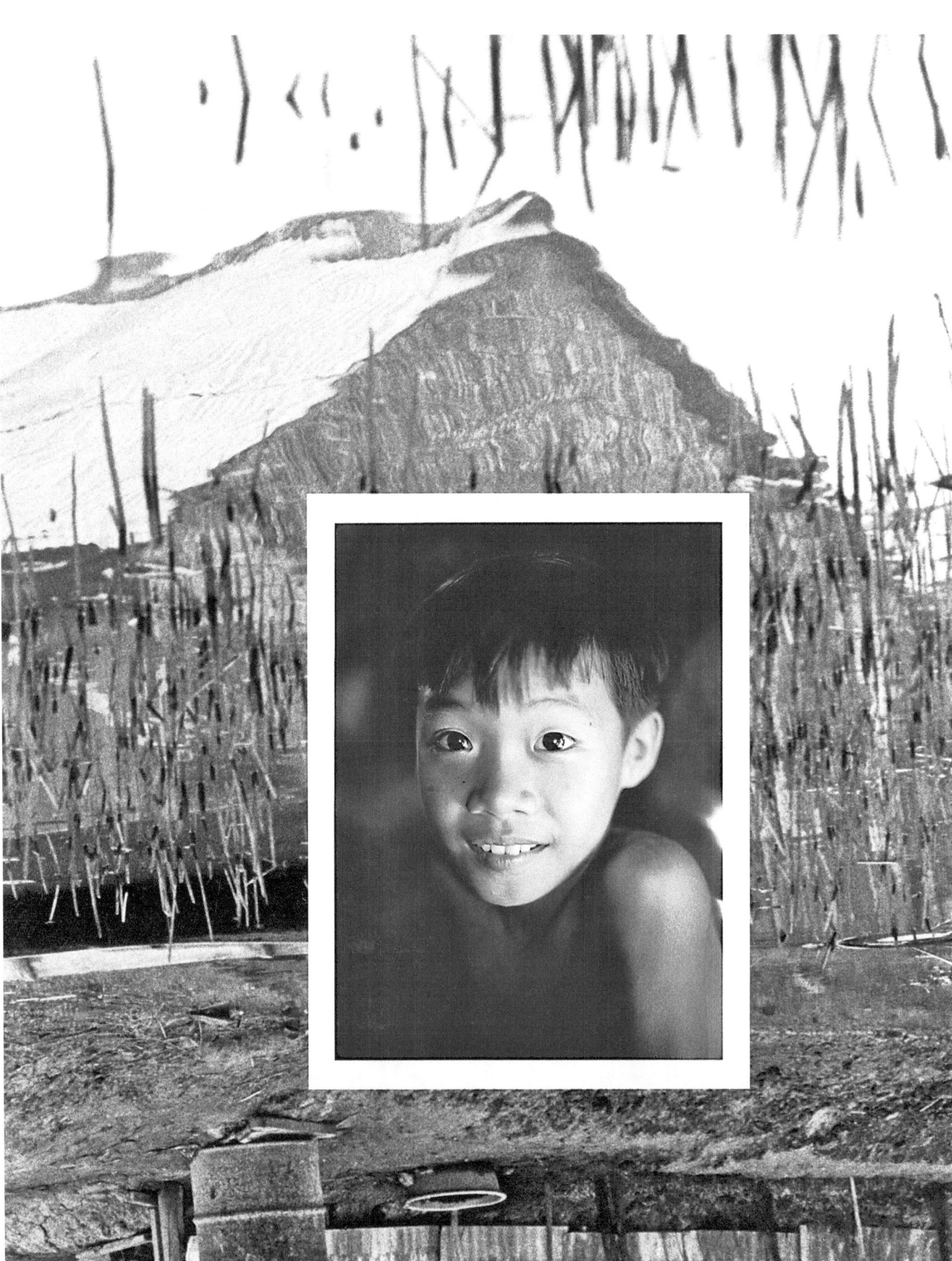

Children were a favorite photographic subject. Little girls were usually shy, but the boys, especially in a group, liked to ham it up for the camera. They all wanted candy and they all seemed to think arm hair was funny.

Kids from the country and smaller villages tended to be more timid and wary of foreign soldiers. Many of the kids from Saigon's hub were downright aggressive. Some were orphans and no doubt a fair share had gravitated to the city because of the war. They begged and picked pockets just to get by. For those kids, charm became a tool for existence and childish exuberance faded as life became more difficult.

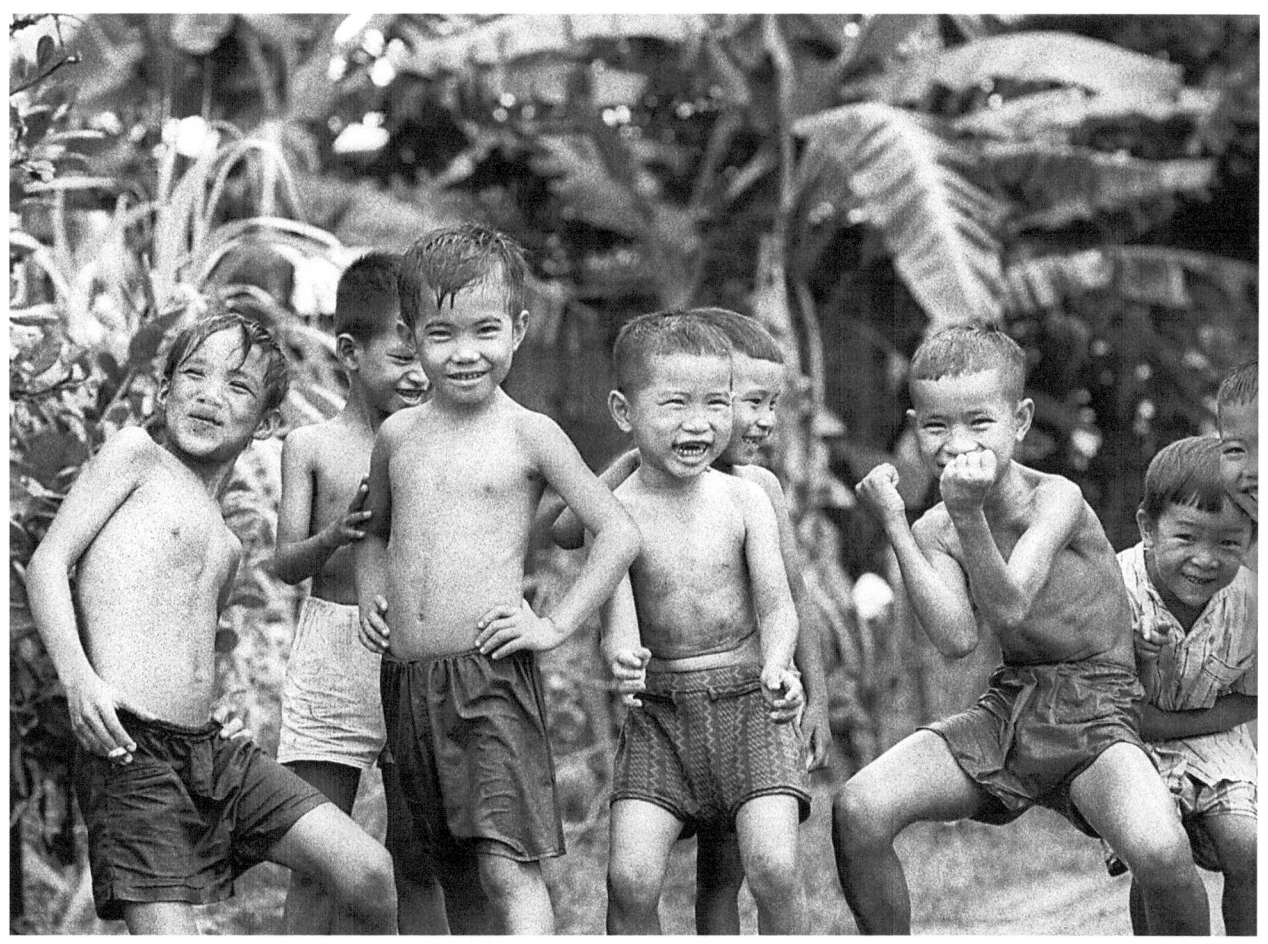

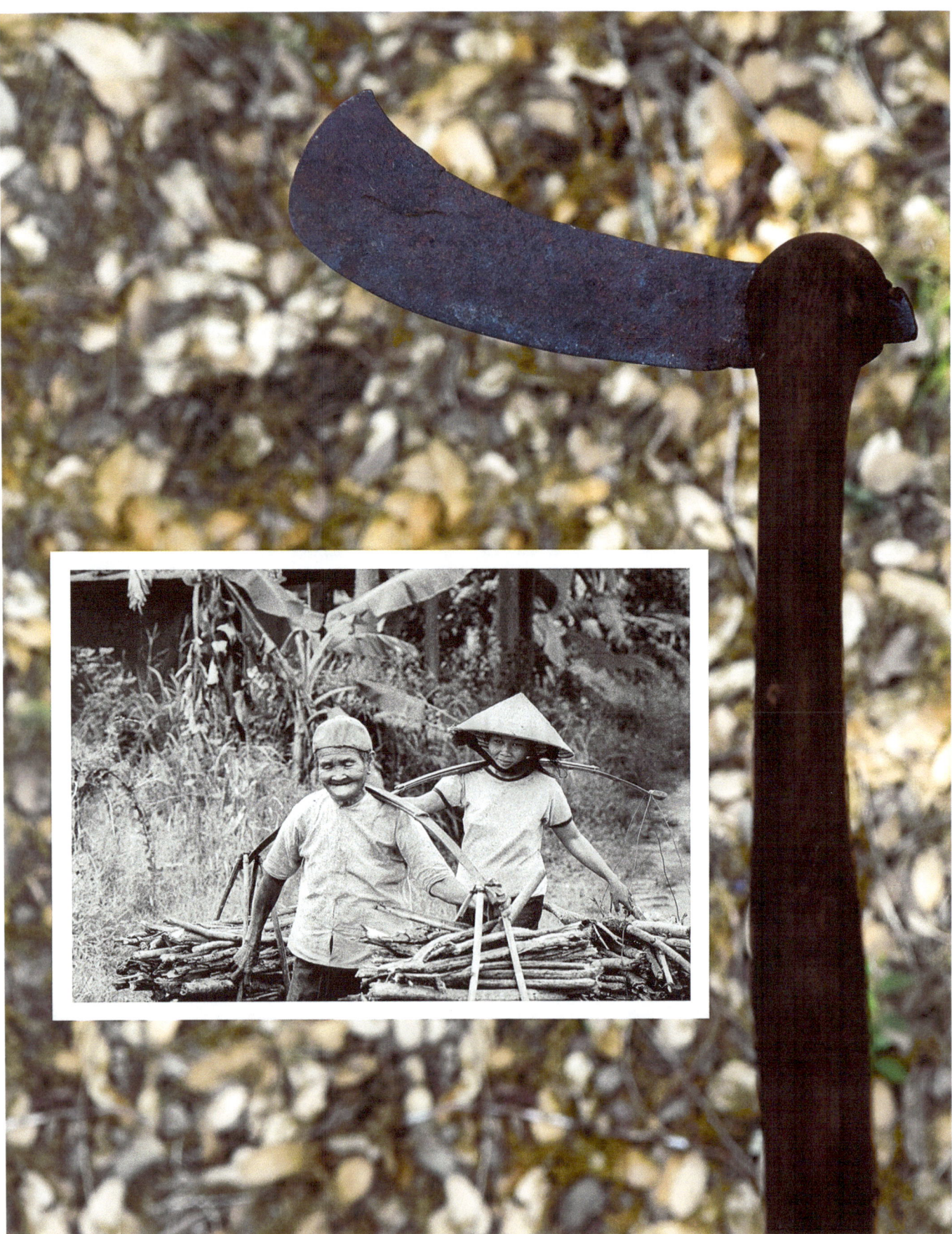

Sometimes I would catch a ride with a convoy and get off at a village to take pictures. On those occasions I could spend the afternoon in the country before hitching a ride back to base.

Naivety is just as blissful as ignorance. The dangers of traveling alone were obvious but the communities I visited seemed benign, like isolated pockets barely touched by war. There was never any planning, and seldom any thought involved; just a quick decision about how to spend some free time.

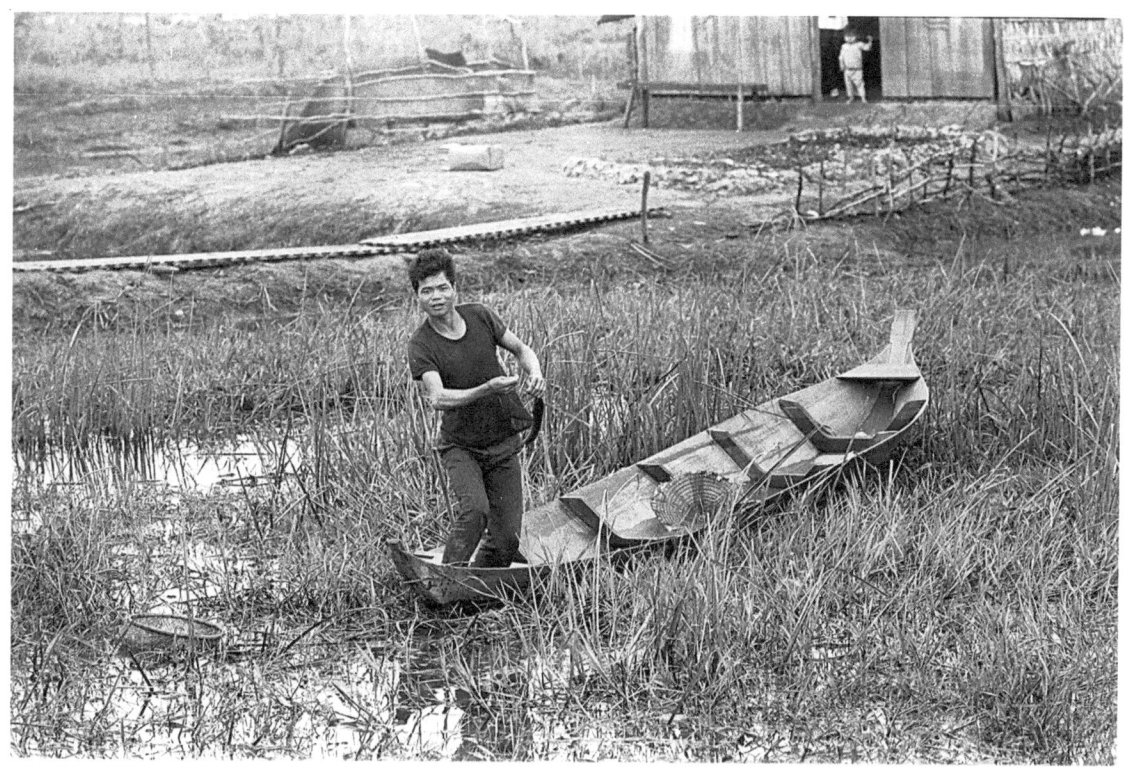

Firebases were where the real soldiers lived when they were not in the bush. The bases were fortified clearings surrounded by concertina wire and claymore mines. In the rainy season they became mud pits.

Hooches (living quarters) were usually dug out of the ground and had sandbags lining the roof and sides. Sometimes they had rats. The grunts that lived there tried to make their quarters as comfortable and utilitarian as possible. Some of the hooches were decorated with pictures from home and had battery powered cassette decks for music. Some were adorned with war trophies.

The fire base hooches I slept in were transient quarters so they were spartan—a cot and something to keep your gear off the ground when it rained. They were nice quiet places to sleep though, unless they were located near a howitzer battery.

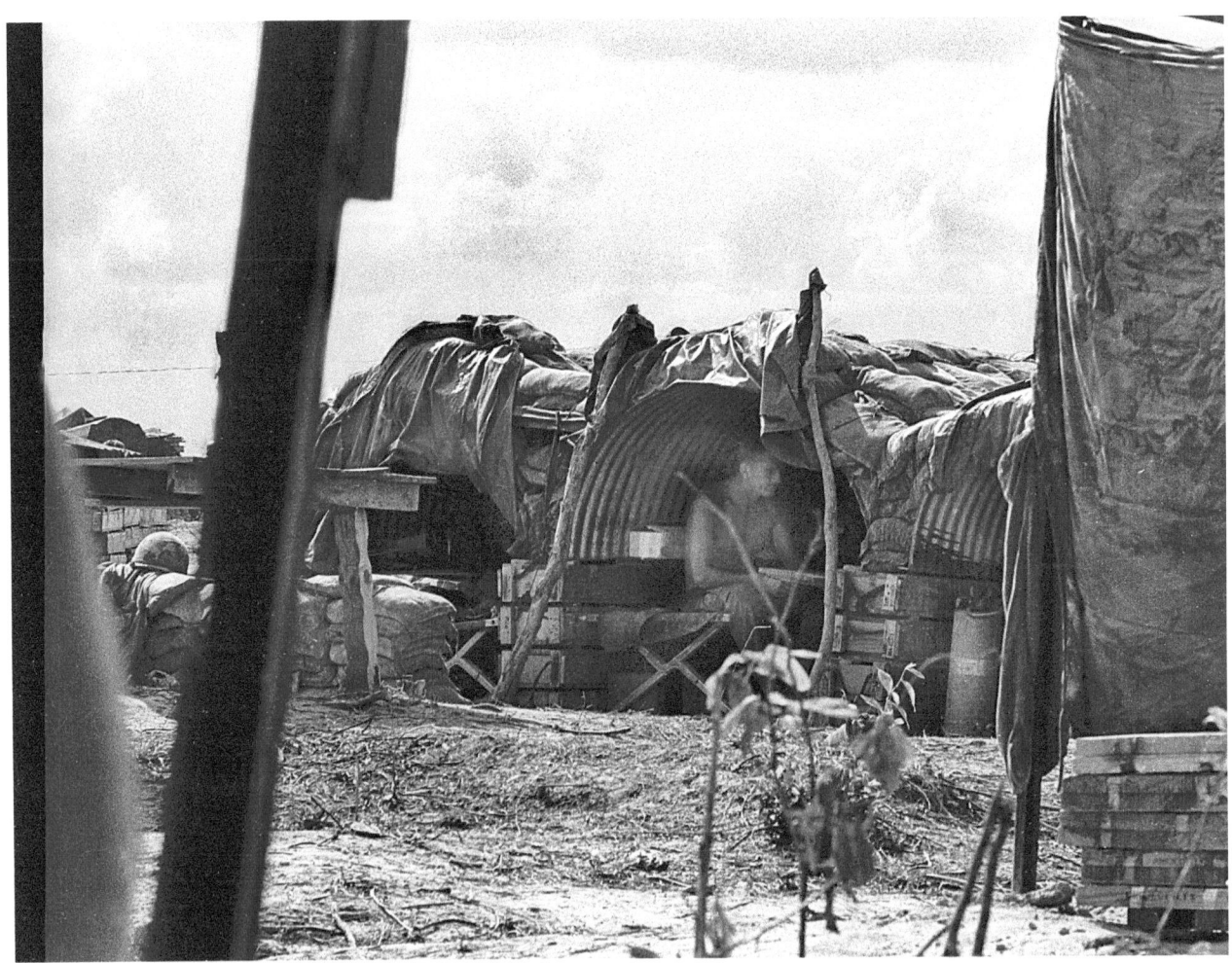

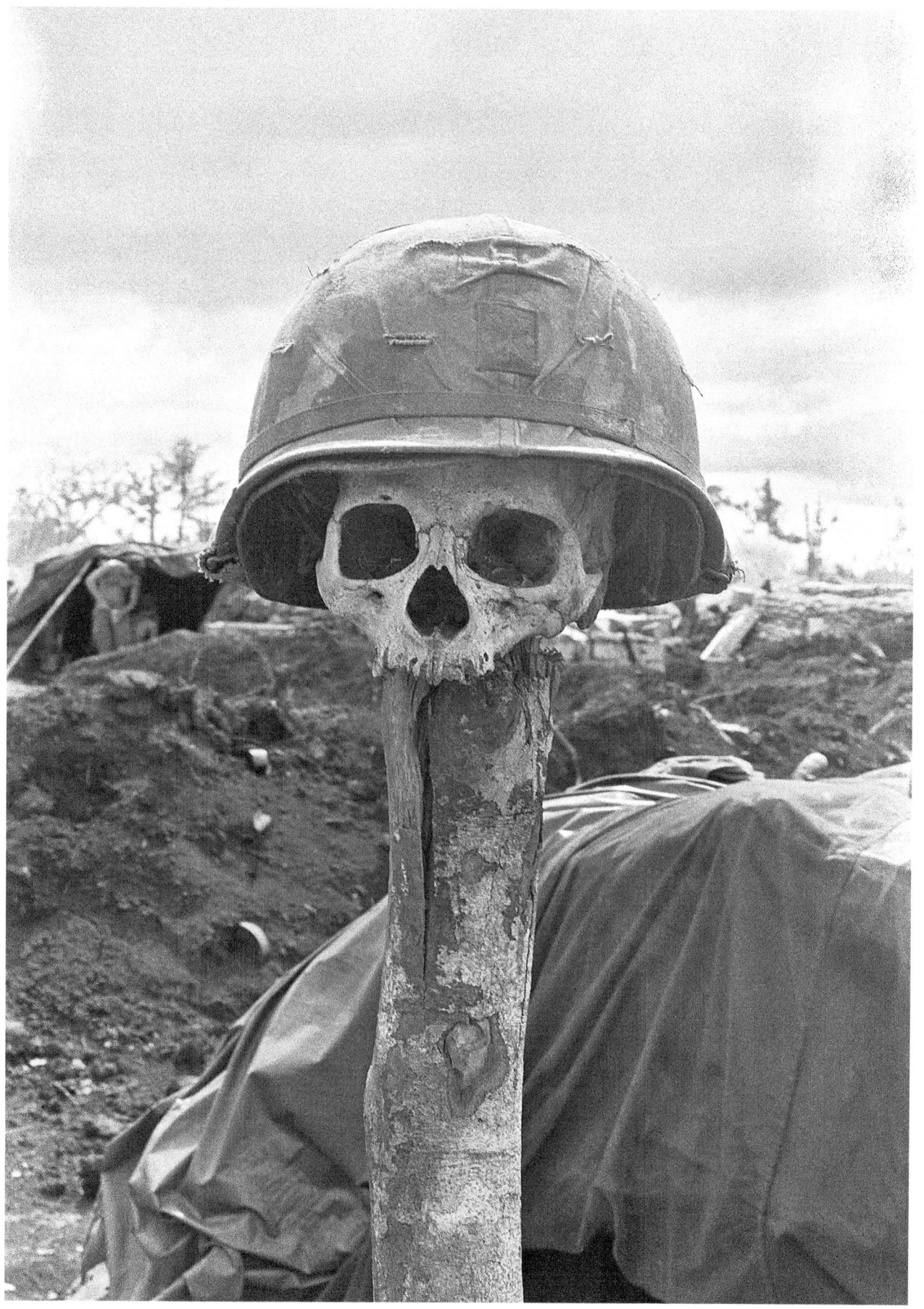

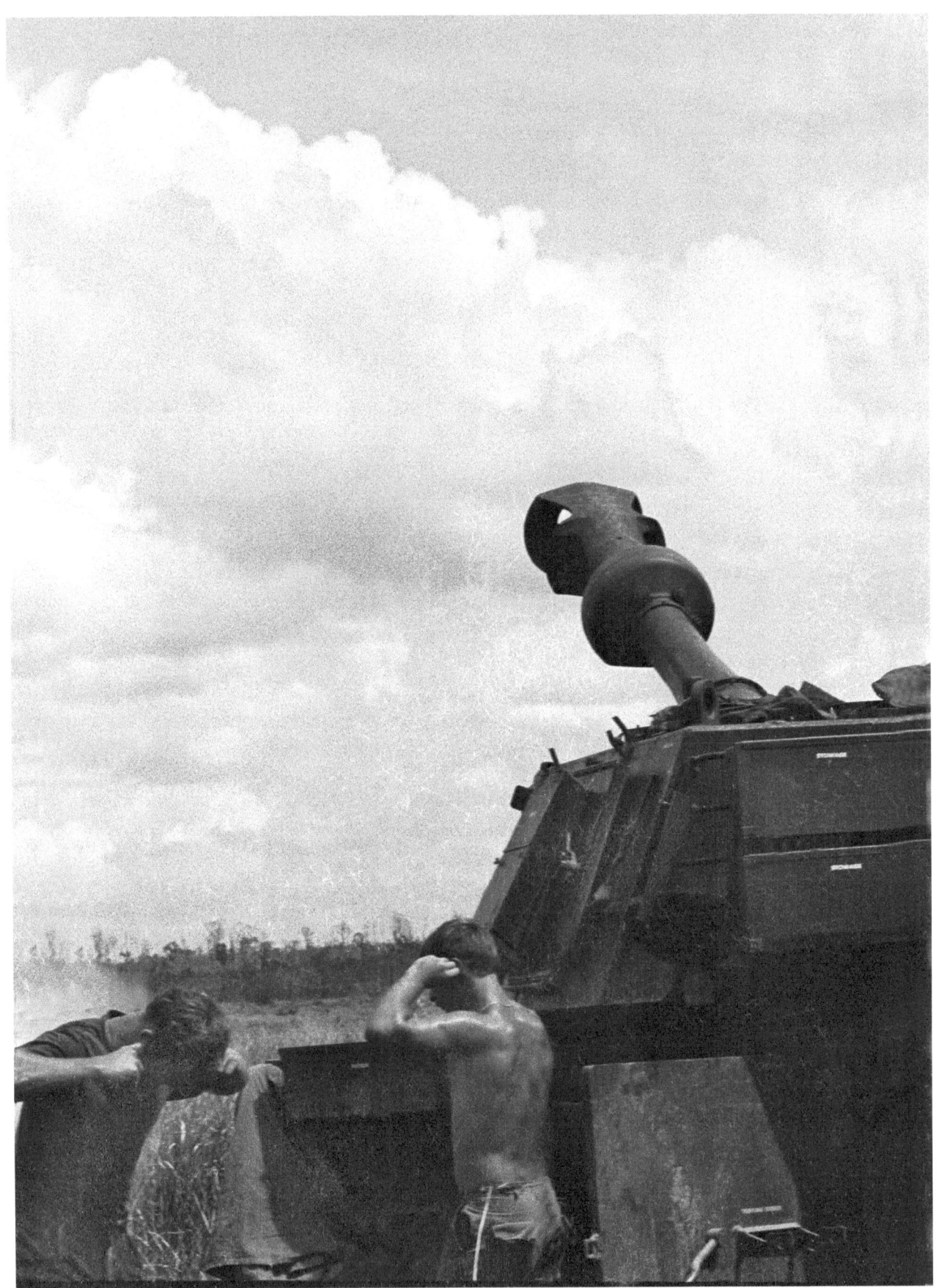

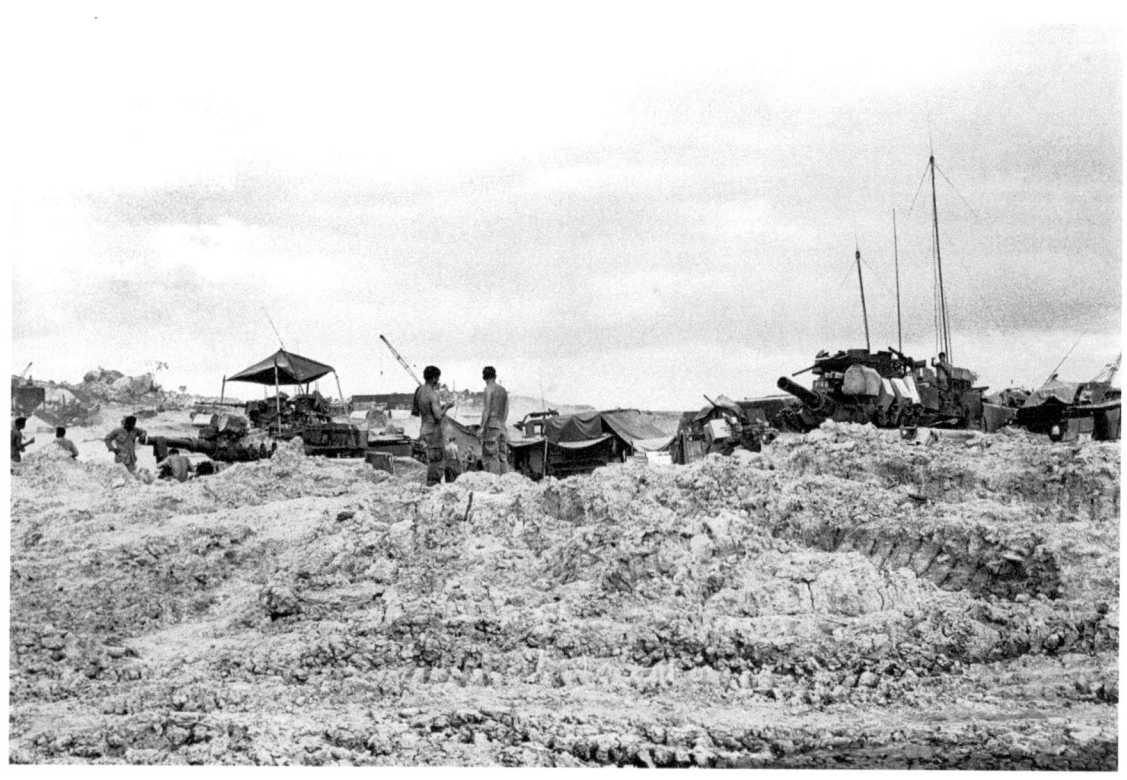

True fire support bases housed artillery to support troops in the bush. From outside the perimeter, a radioman could call in coordinates of enemy troops and our artillery would pound the area. Some fire support bases had howitzer units that would lob shells into the countryside at odd intervals throughout the night. The noise level around howitzer batteries was deafening and the concussion of outgoing shells raised the dust and sleeping soldiers several inches off a cot.

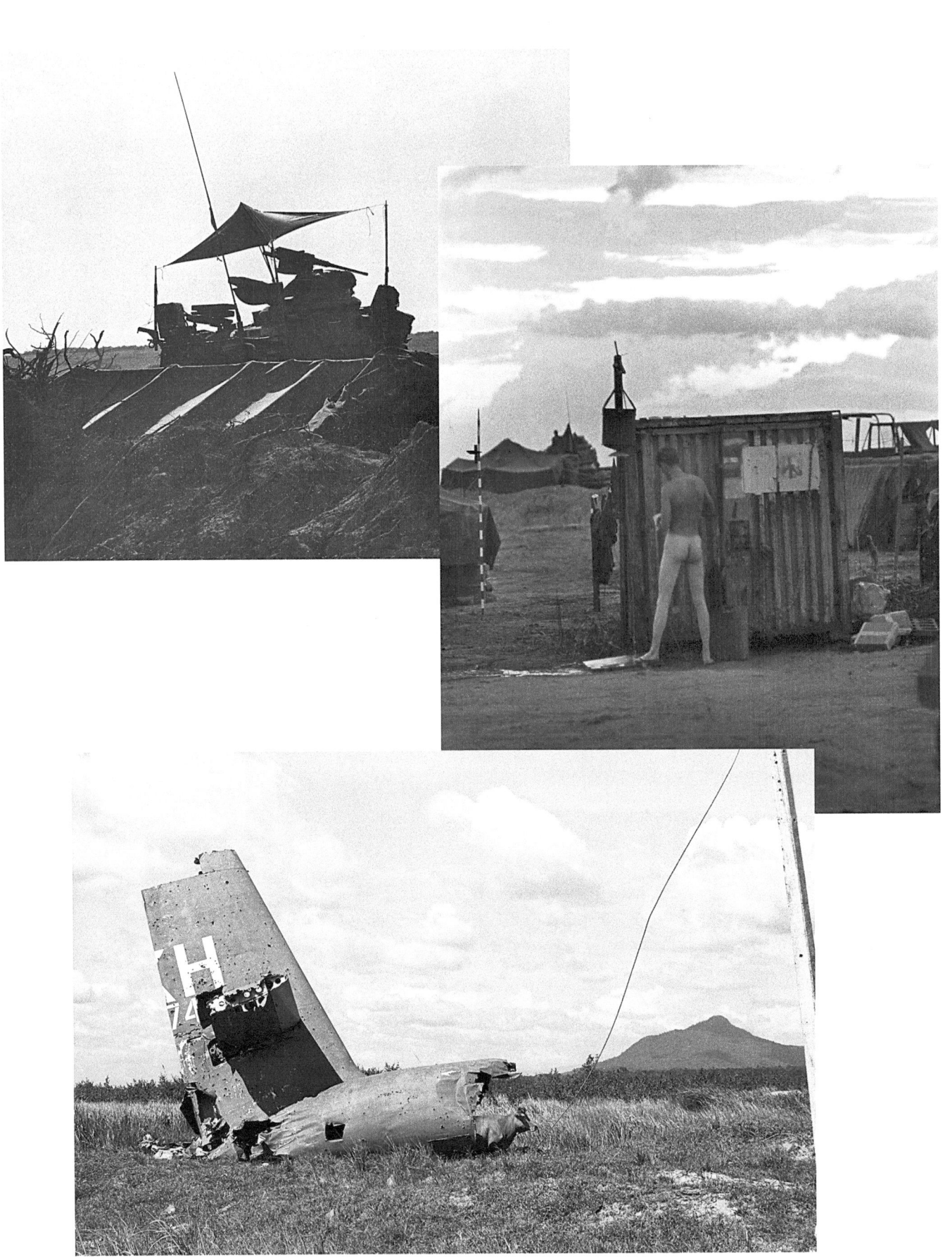

Showers were hanging buckets with holes poked in the bottom. Urinals were piss tubes jutting out of the ground. Toilets were outhouses over a cut off 50-gallon drum to collect the waste. Diesel fuel was poured over the feces and burned on a daily basis.

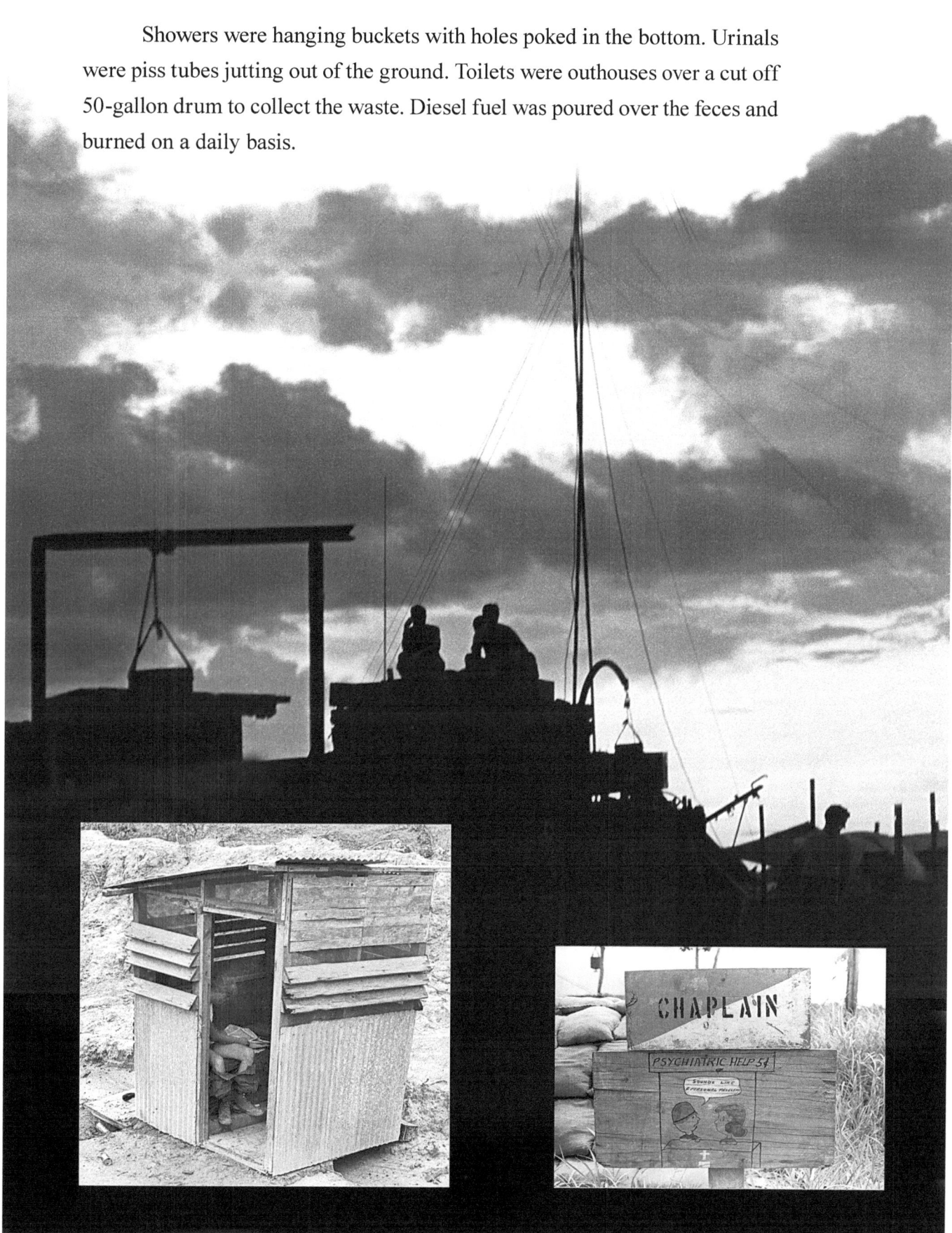

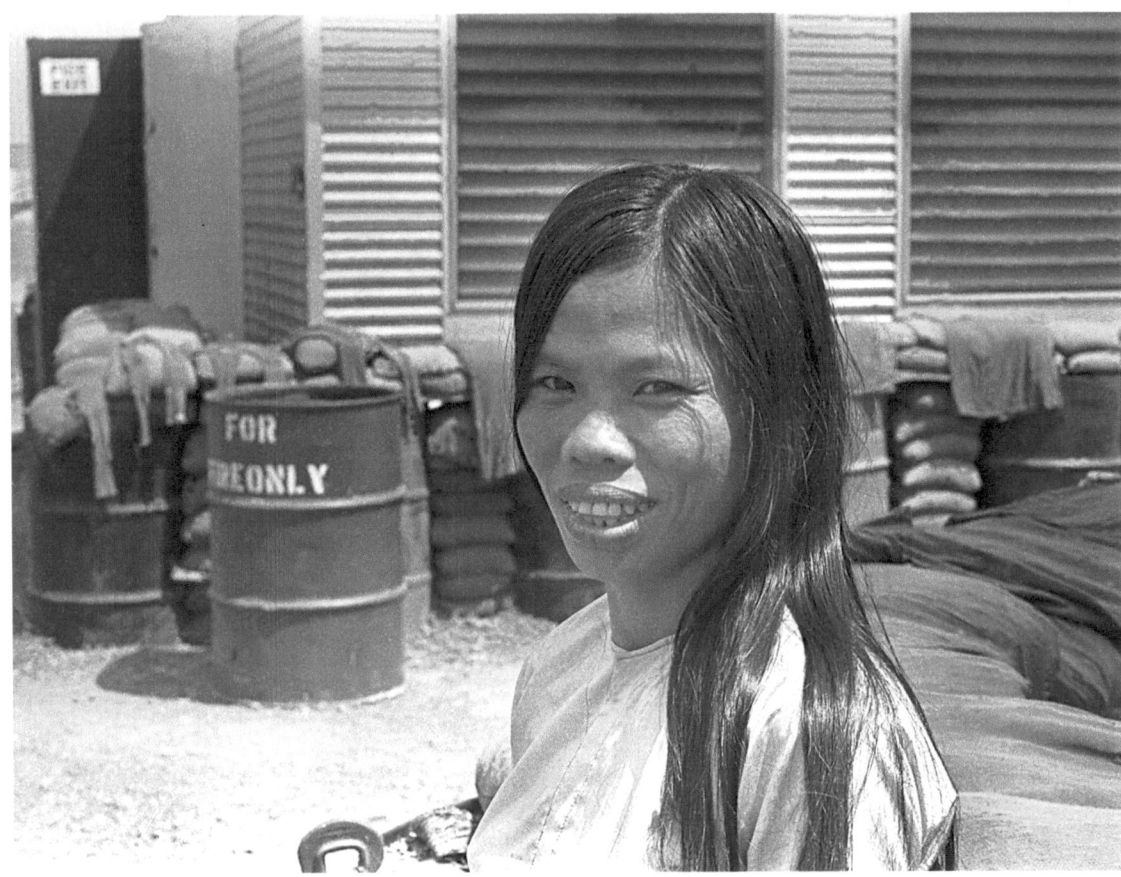

Long Binh, Cam Ranh Bay and some of the larger Army posts were on the other end of the scale. They were sprawling complexes with real showers, flush toilets, and barracks with beds. There were craft and entertainment centers, snack bars and post exchanges. They were comfortable and semi-secure.

They also had rules and regulations and a high concentration of officers that expected to be saluted. Base camps might get more incoming artillery but nobody made you spit shine your boots. The very things a soldier had to do at Long Binh were indicators of a neophyte on a firebase.

The U.S. military employed Vietnamese civilians to perform our housekeeping chores, etc. Before sunrise they would gather outside the main gates, waiting to be let in. Sometimes I could smell their cooking fires and hear them laughing and talking. From the "momasan" who washed our uniforms, to "Willie the shit burner" who literally burned vats of military feces, the workers seemed happier than they should be. Often they seemed more content than those of us who would someday be flying back to the United States of America—to the place of their dreams.

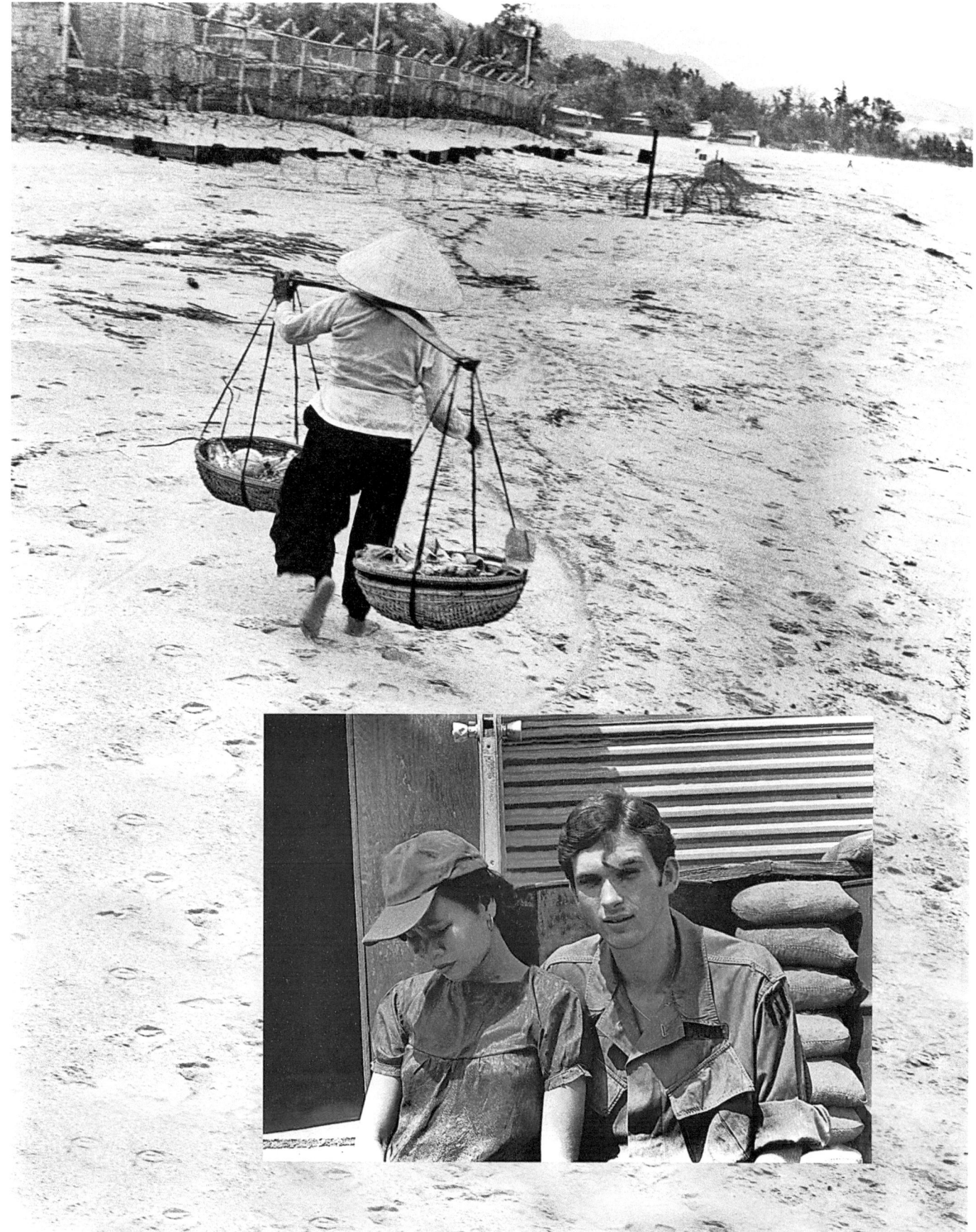

Saigon's major thoroughfares were clogged with all sorts of traffic. Bicycle drawn cyclos competed with cars, motorcycles and Army deuce and a half's. Right of way seemed to be determined by vehicle size.

The sidewalks were just as congested. Refugees and beggars, civilians and soldiers all competed for space. Navigating downtown Saigon required ones full attention. Children would crowd around solitary servicemen, tugging at their uniforms and begging candy and cigarettes. Sometimes a tiny hand would slip into his pocket.

Young prostitutes would dash out of doorways to snatch a boonie hat, playing keep away while trying to entice the soldier inside. Men beckoned from alleyways offering money exchanges, girls and drugs. Black market bazaars sold US military items and other goods. It was the place to buy back the poncho liner that was stolen the day before.

Saigon was a dichotomy. It was a good place to hide from Army regulations, but scary without military protection. In the company of friends it was an adventure. Alone it could be a frightening place to relax. The main boulevards of Saigon were filled with images but I usually held my camera tight against my chest for fear of losing it. It is a reflection of my own insecurities that I have few pictures of that area.

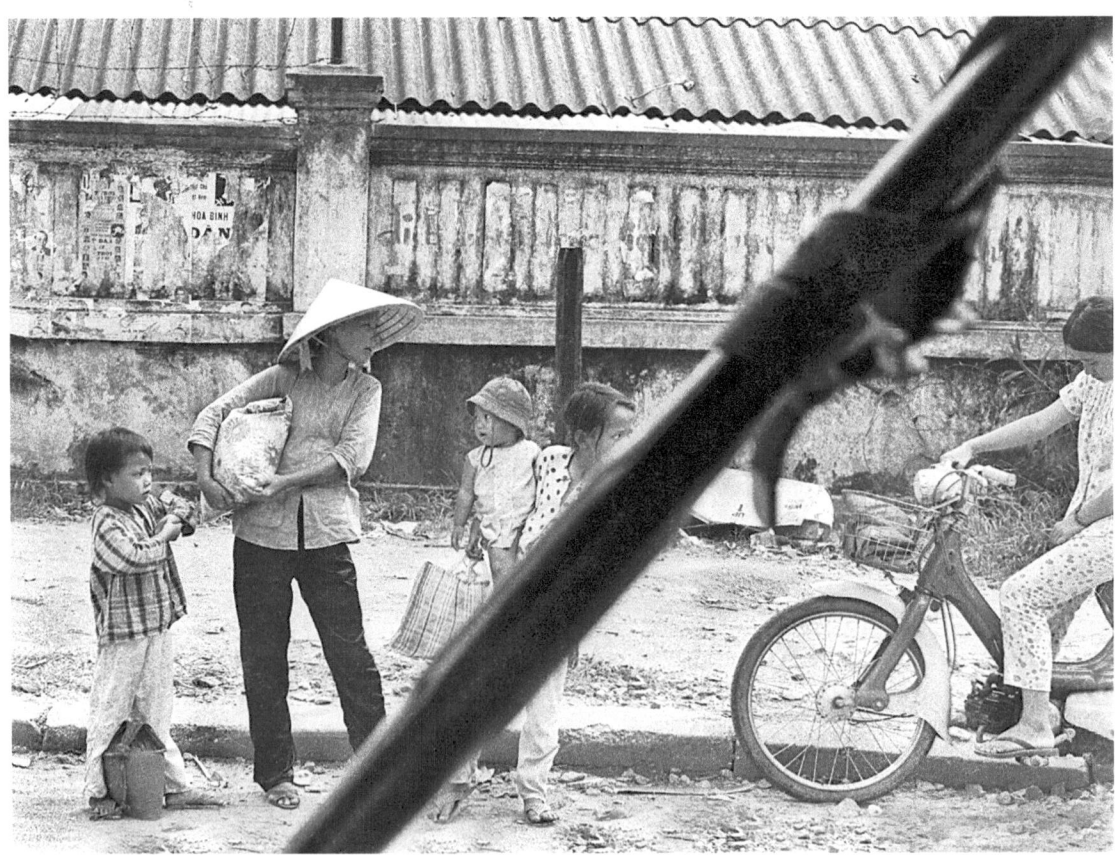

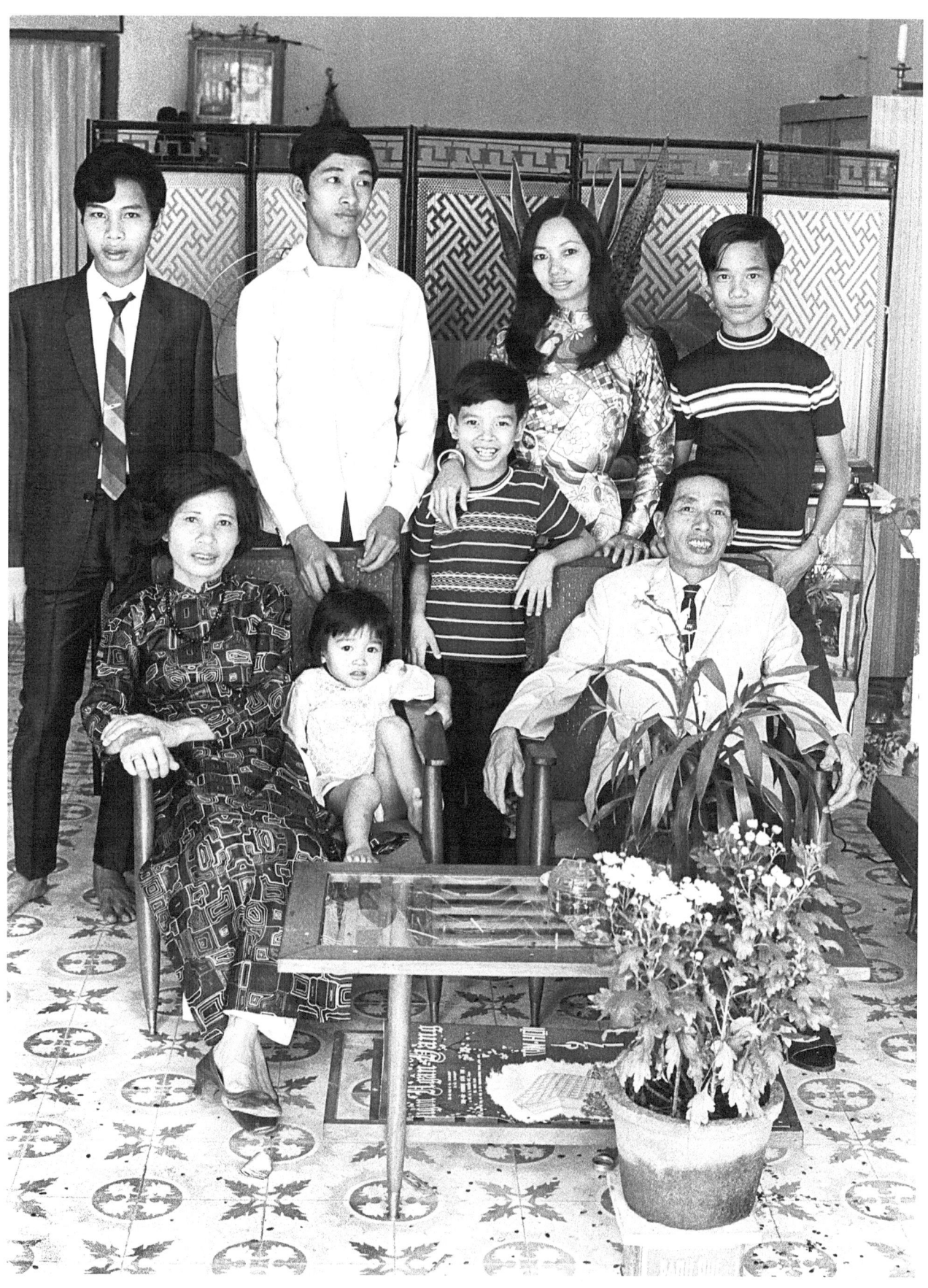

The back streets of Cholon, the Chinese section of Saigon were less frenetic. They were unpaved and less traveled by four wheel traffic. The area smelled of cooking fires and food stalls, with a subtle undertone of sewage.

I met a girl named Han who lived in Cholon. She showed me a few places around the city and tried to teach me to negotiate with the vendors. Once she helped me buy a porcelain vase for my mother.

We communicated in a mixture of French, English and Vietnamese words that sounded like a form of baby talk. She used to tell me, "I love you beaucoup. You love me peti," (petite). "You butterfly, I die."

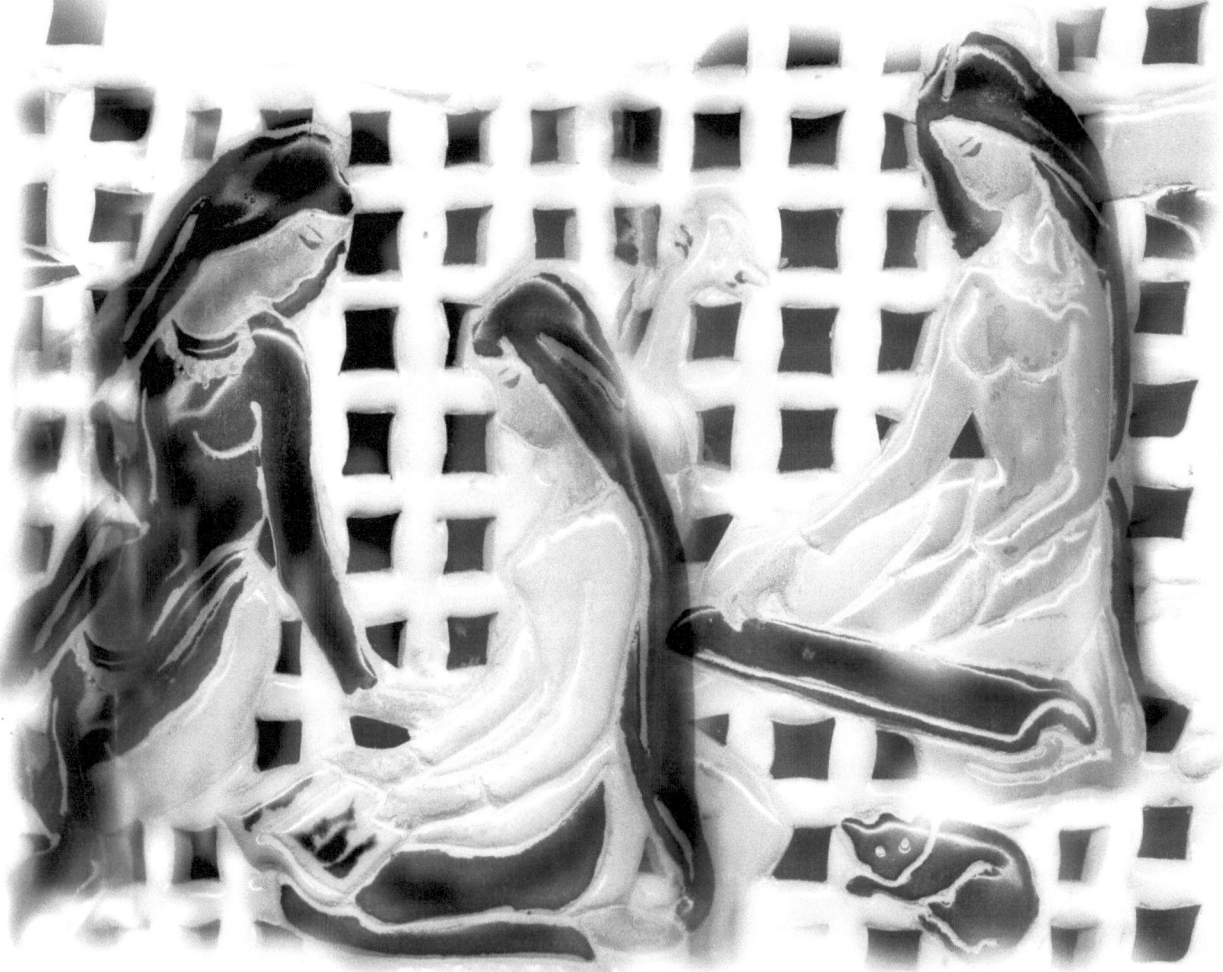

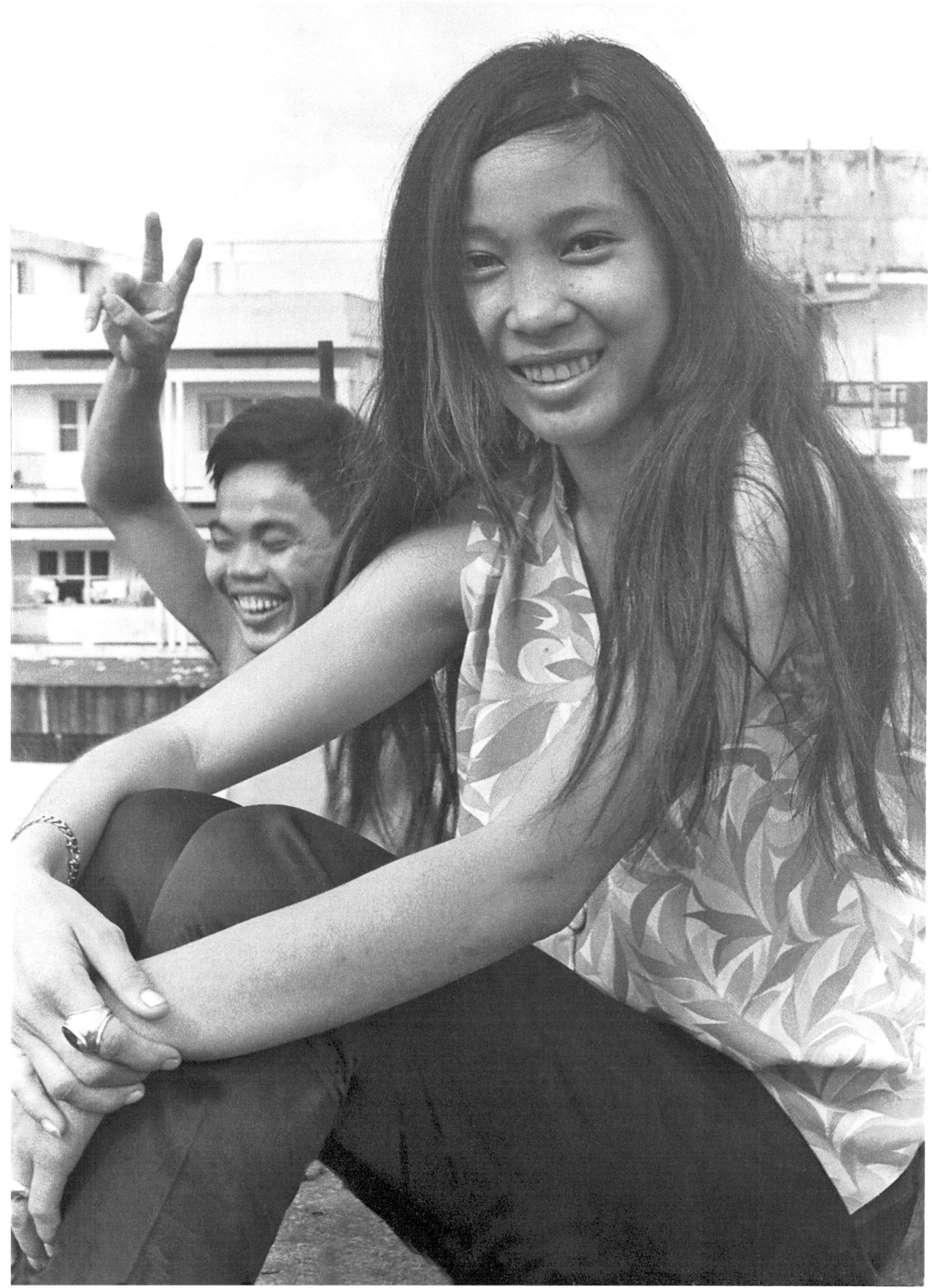

Han had a brother who was AWOL from the ARVN—a South Vietnamese Army deserter. He and his friend were "cowboys." In its broadest sense the moniker described any Vietnamese hooligan, but these guys specialized in mobile theft. One of them drove a motorcycle while the other, holding tight to his partner's waist, reached out and snatched cameras, wristwatches, etc. from their unsuspecting victims.

Cyclo passengers were their usual prey. A cyclo is an open air cart propelled by a bicycle. A cyclo passenger often had his arm casually draped across the side of the cart. If the arm was wearing a wristwatch or camera strap, a cowboy team could speed up from behind, rip the item off and disappear into traffic. I was sharing a cyclo ride with a friend one day when he lost his watch to cowboys that quickly zigzagged through the maze of vehicles, and were gone.

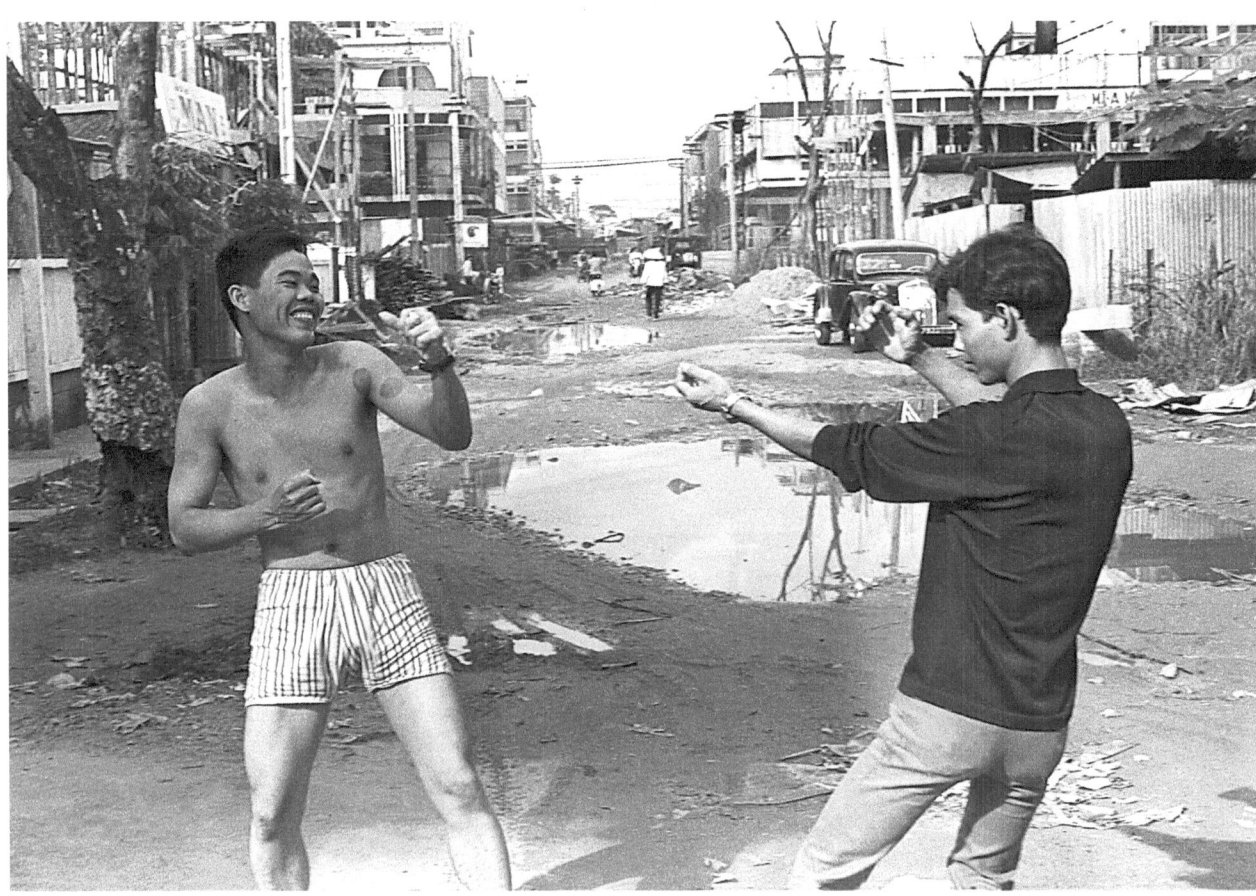

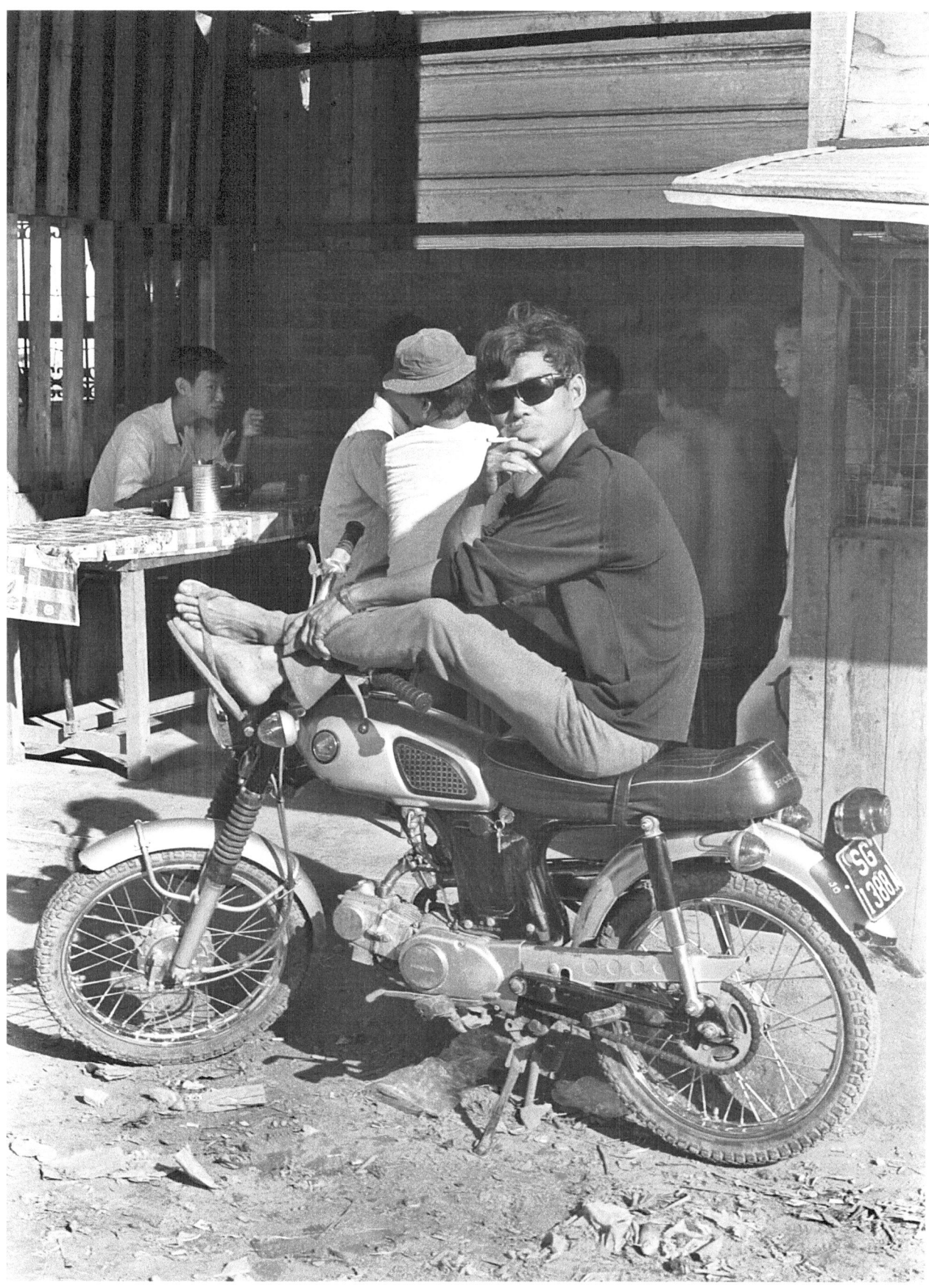

There was a communal apartment in Cholon that I shared with some other correspondents. As far as I know, none of us ever managed to stay there more than two or three nights a month, and seldom at the same time. There were a few bargirls that lived in the building, and although the proprietors ran a wholesome establishment with rules to the contrary, sex and drugs did occur.

The place was clean and secure with a second floor balcony that overlooked a dirt street. A low cinder block wall surrounded the balcony so it was a good place to relax outside without feeling overly exposed.

Most of what I remember about that apartment happened on the outside of the balcony wall. One night there was what looked like a Vietnamese block party. I'm not sure what time of year it was, so I can not equate the event with a festival. Anyway, a large bonfire was blazing in the middle of the street and on top was a dead ox, head and tail intact; fur on fire.

The animal had a spread eagle rigor mortis appearance that made him look like he was frozen in time, trying to leap over the fire. I shot a couple rolls of slide film, and lost them when I returned to the states.

The following pictures were all taken from that balcony, but if not for their negatives, all I would remember about that place is the ox in the fire.

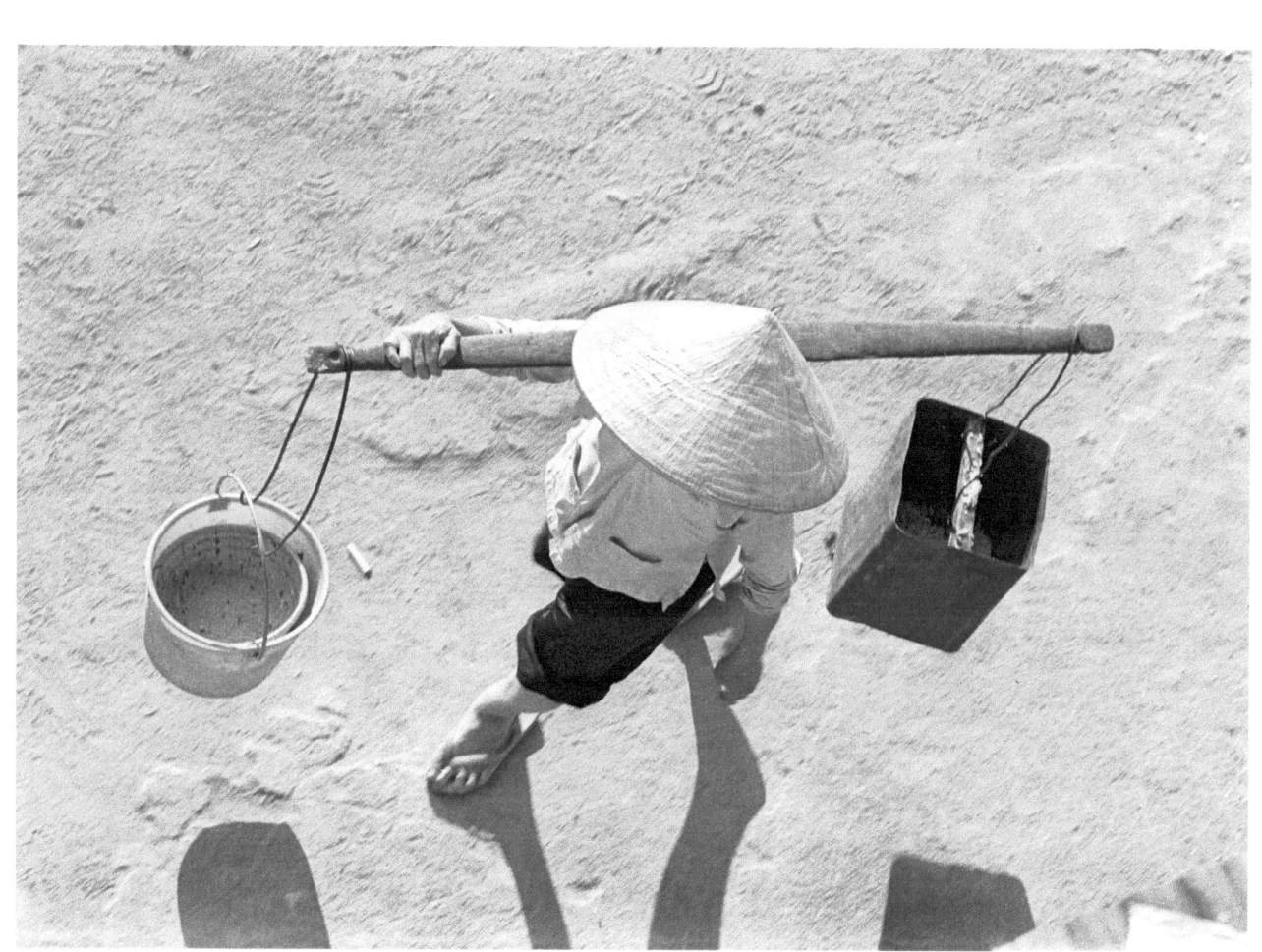

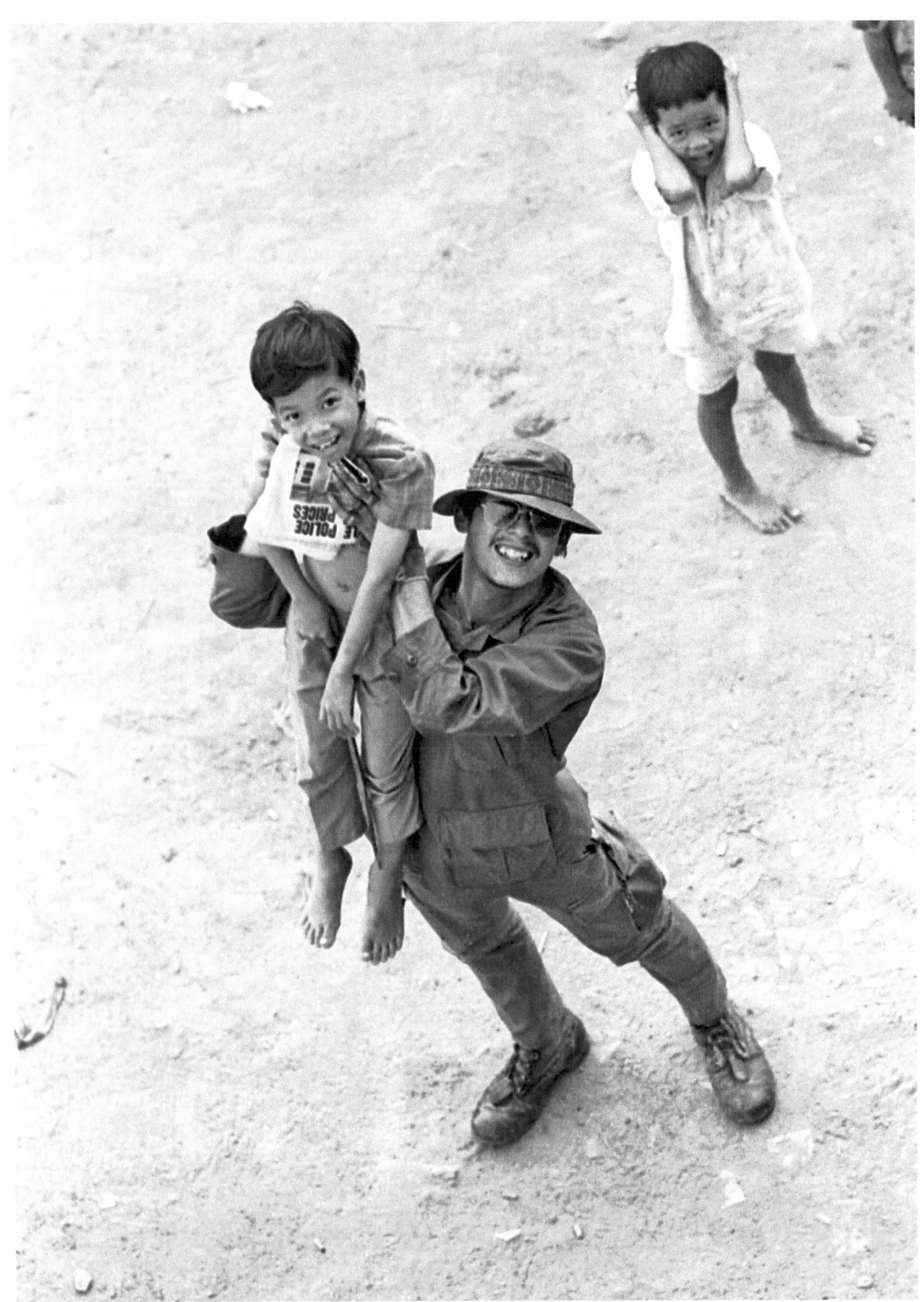

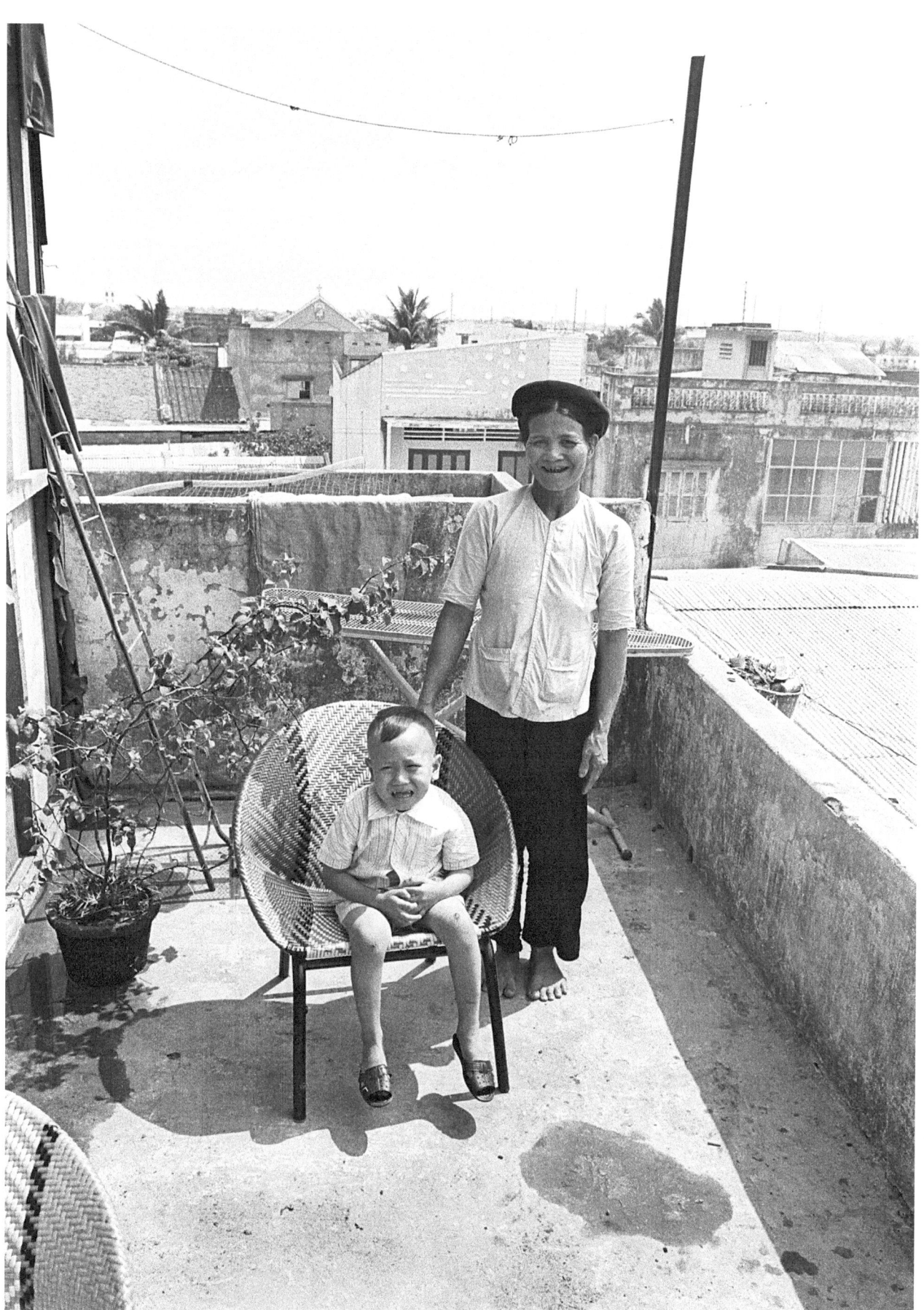

Sometime around October of 1970 I was traveling with a platoon of 1st Cavalry grunts when they found a hooch full of rice hidden in the jungle. The lieutenant radioed its location to headquarters and it was decided to search the area before destroying the cache.

Not far from the rice hooch we stumbled onto a small Mantagnard village. Two men carrying AK47s came into view and a very brief firefight ensued. One NVA soldier was killed and at least one other escaped, leaving a blood trail. We followed the trail until it disappeared but the guy got away. Later while rifling through the dead man's few possessions, two of the "grunts" got into a friendly argument about who killed the gook. Both soldiers claimed the kill and the argument lasted much longer than the firefight.

We questioned the few villagers we could find. There were less than a dozen old men and women. They all had shorn grey hair, like ragged crew cuts, and the men had elongated ear lobes with large holes in the middle. They said the NVA were bad people who stole their food and children.

We torched the village and escorted the Montagnards back to Firebase Bandit for further questioning and relocation. The next day a helicopter flew in from MACV headquarters with enough ice cream for everyone in the platoon. It was local policy at the time to reward every confirmed kill with ice cream.

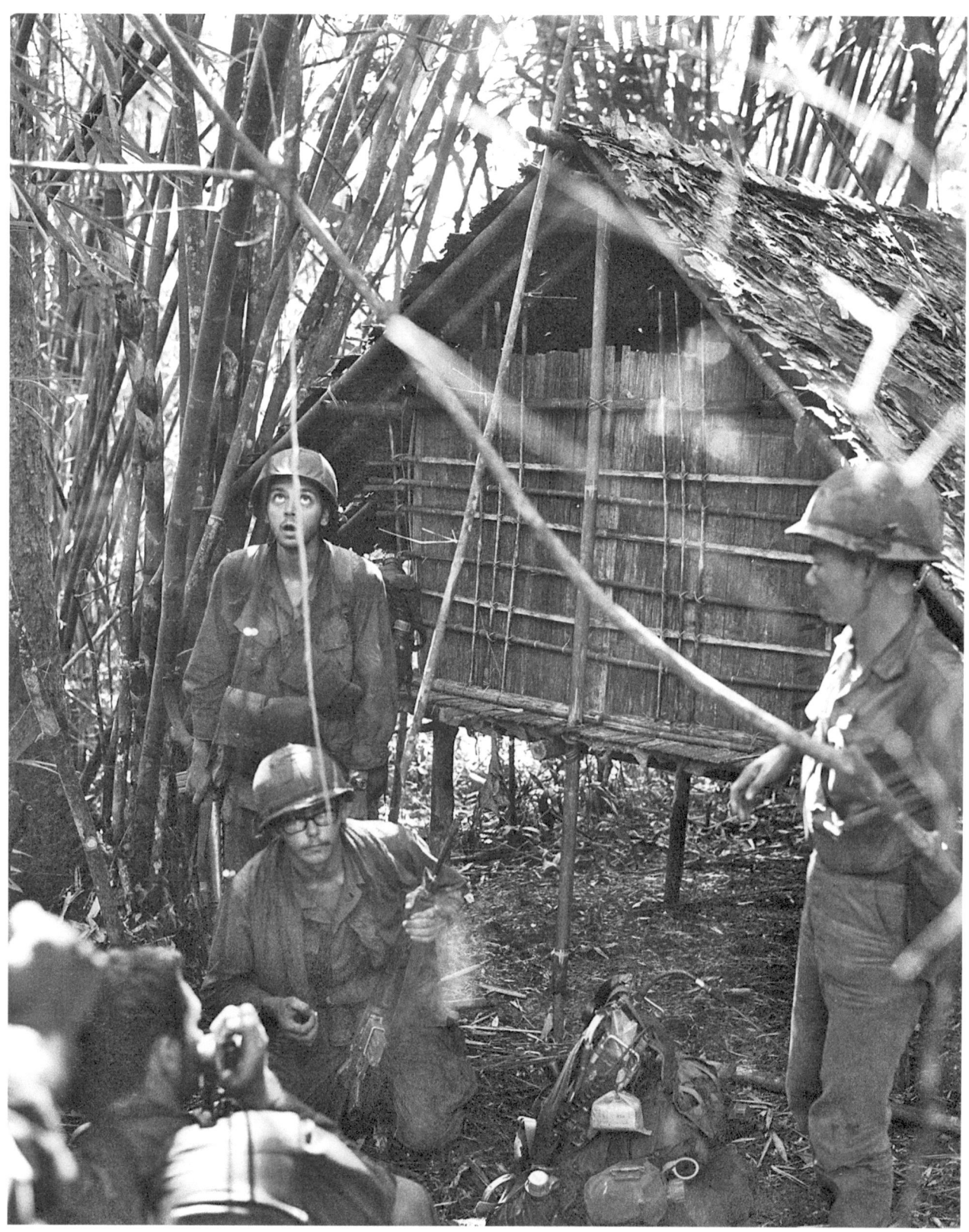

The dead enemy soldier is one of the few pictures I have from the Montagnard village. I shot most of the episode on color slide film, then lost all my slides after returning to the US. I found the image of the dead soldier in a slide duplicating attachment many years later. It is the only image left of my color work.

The rectangular thing at the bottom right is his wallet. It contained a picture of his girlfriend, or maybe his wife. Whoever she was, she would never see him again. I wish I had taken a picture of her picture. It would make the dead guy look more "of this world," which he was, just before this picture was taken.

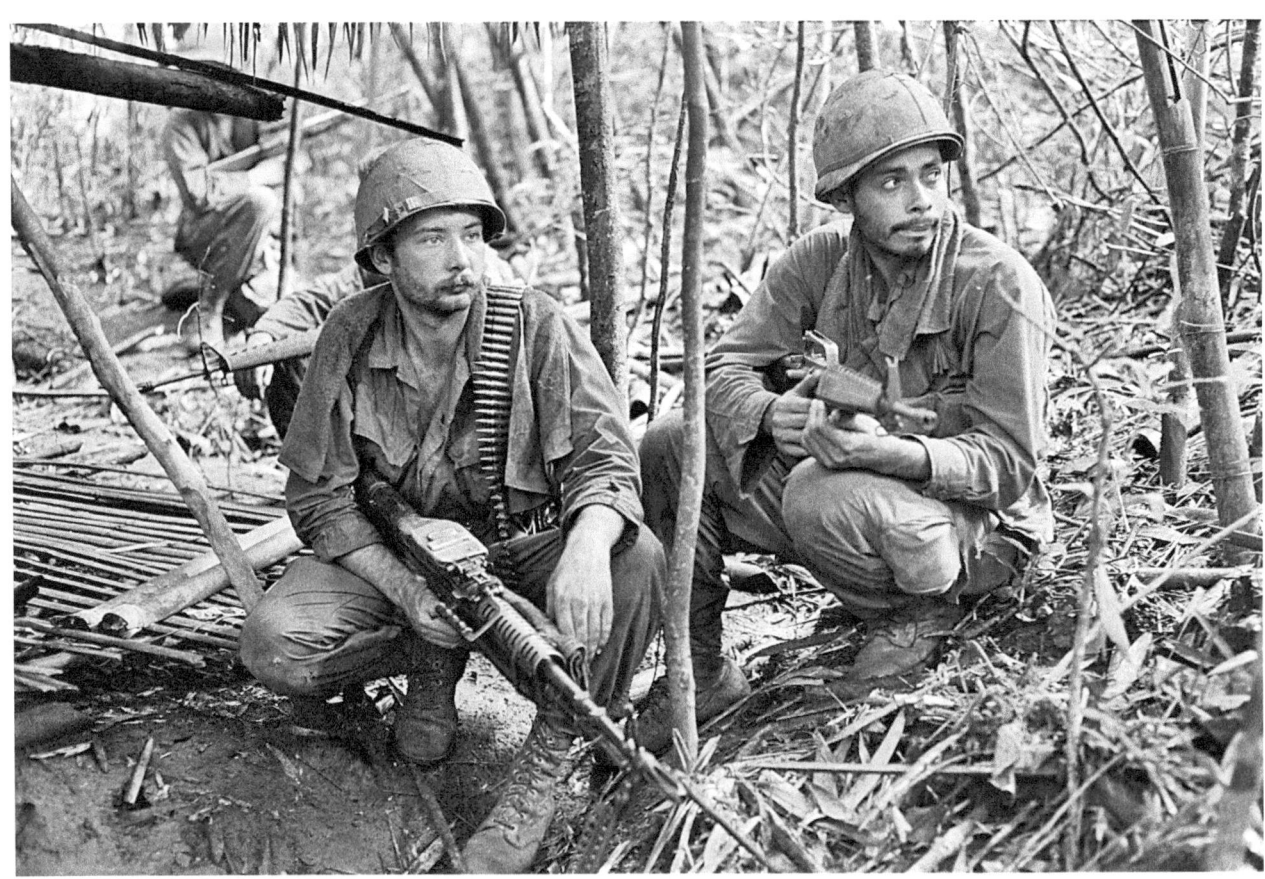

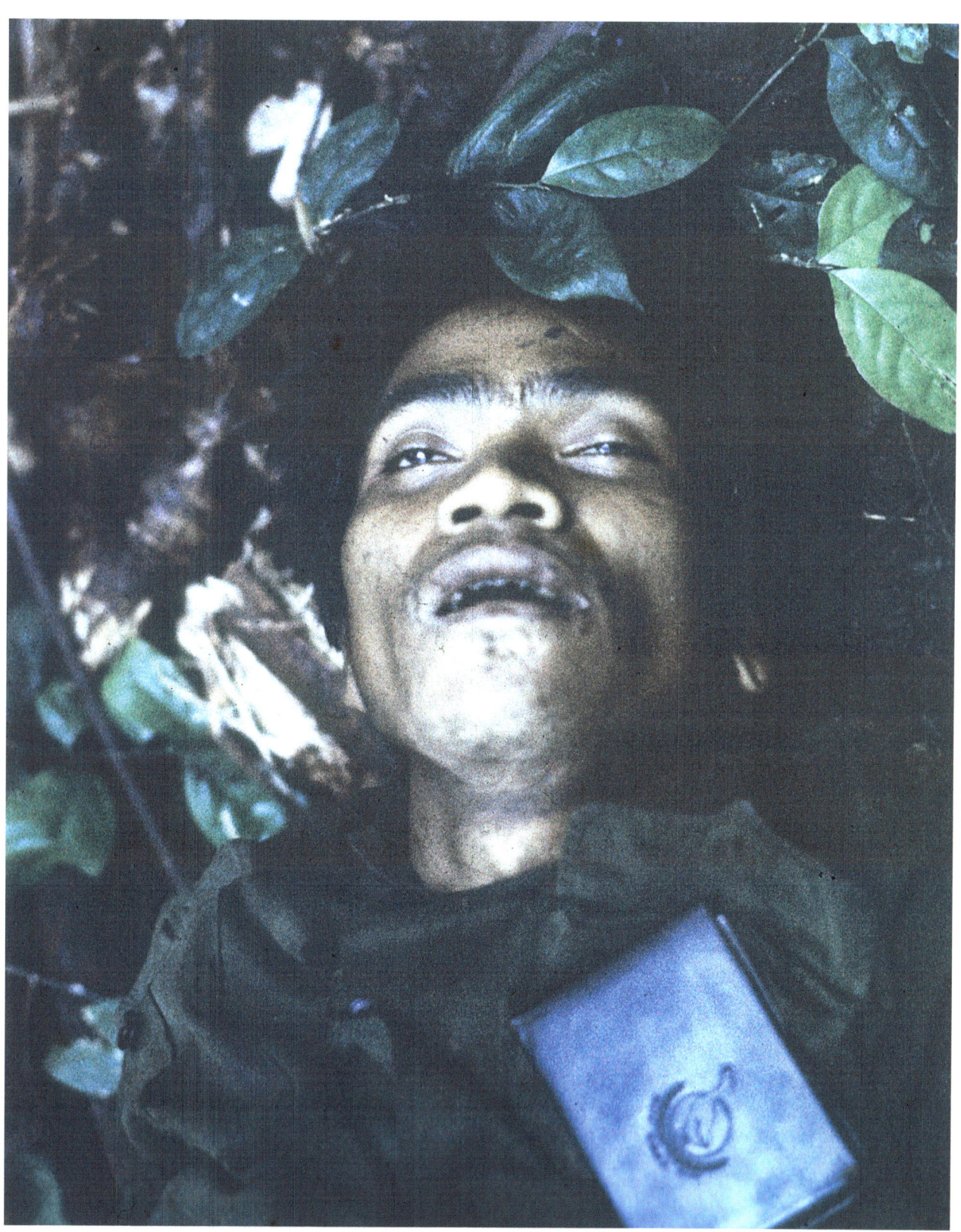

Within a day or two of Christmas, 1970, some grunts discovered an abandoned VC camp. They marked the spot with yellow smoke so a helicopter flying over the dense jungle could make out the location. Smoke grenade colors were predetermined to keep the choppers from being lured into an ambush by the enemy.

In the shafts of light that penetrated the jungle canopy, the yellow had a bright neon quality. The spears of light looked like multiple holograms rising through the dull shadows of vegetation, and the smoke drifting upward made the vertical shapes of the jungle waver and dance. There were some places in the canopy where the vegetation thinned and smoke rushed through them like it was trying to escape.

The chopper hovered close overhead with a tape recorder blasting out "Jungle Bells," reminding us of the season. It was a bad recording and a silly play on words that might or might not have made some of us feel better. I don't remember. I do remember that it came from a cleaner, fresher world and it made me envious for not being in the place it came from.

All that remained of the camp were a few low bamboo sleeping platforms and some monkey skulls—dinner remnants.

The camp was located in an expanse of swamp and jungle between Saigon and the Cambodian border. It is infested with mosquitoes and leeches and apparently harbors some monkeys.

The area has been a hideout for Vietnamese bandits as well as religious and political outlaws for hundreds of years. In 1970 it is where the enemy hid from and occasionally harassed the good guys. It was an inhospitable terrain in which to conduct "search and destroy" missions. It must have been a much worse place to hide from them.

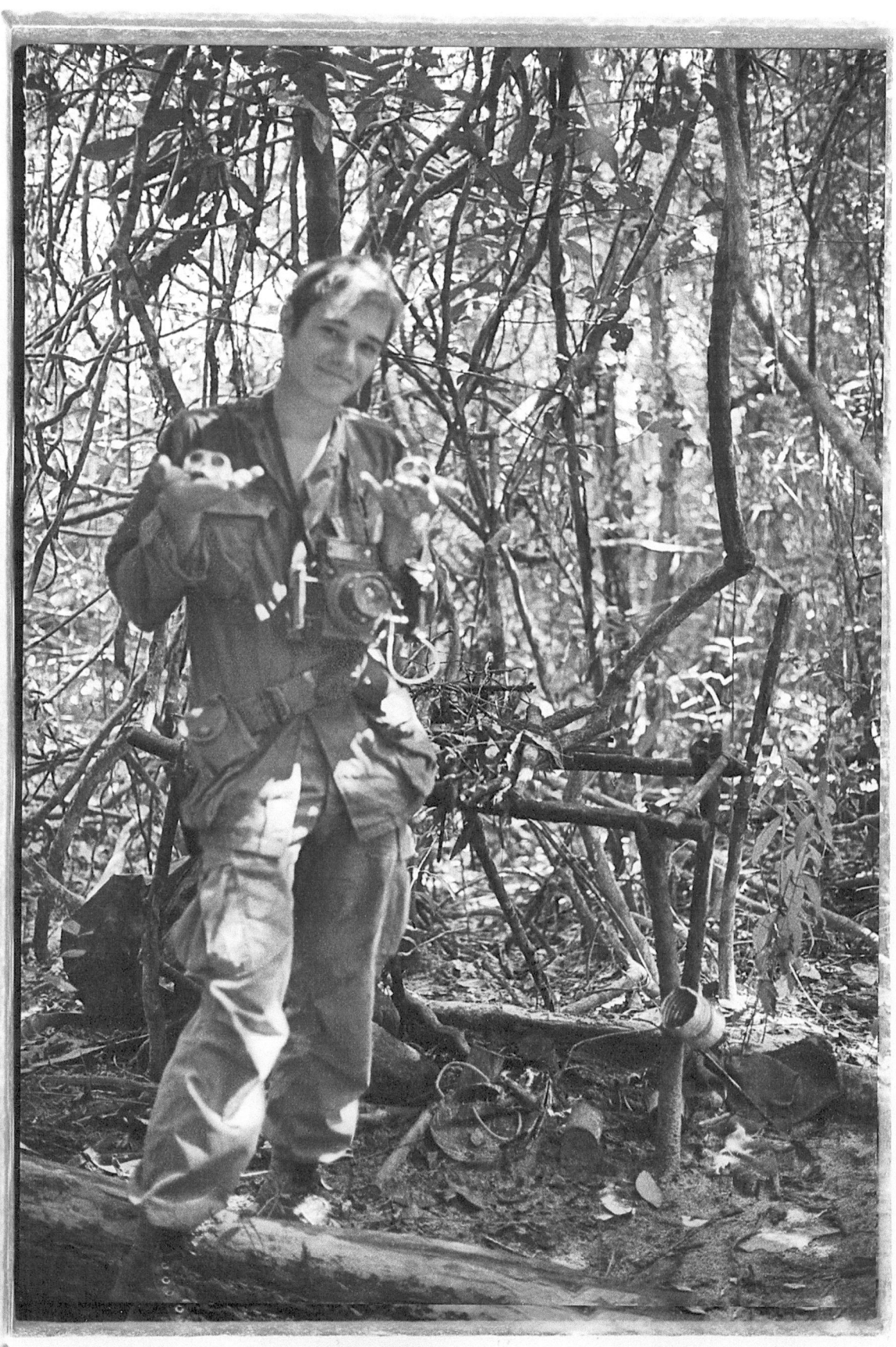

Once, I rode with a convoy of fuel barges, (LCMs), down the Mekong and out into the South China Sea. A US Navy ship loaded us with helicopter fuel, which we transported back inland.

The journey down river was relaxed and almost recreational. Traveling back up country the barges were full and sluggish, and we expected an ambush. In areas of the river that the convoy was most vulnerable, the men stayed at their duty stations and I was told to keep a low profile on the LCMs upper deck. The top deck was a small open area surrounded by sandbags, about three levels high. Inside the sandbags were comic books, Playboy Magazines, an M-60, an M-79 grenade launcher, and ammunition for both weapons.

When the ambush happened our boat was raked with machine gun fire that ricocheted off the steel plating. I could see tracers flying out of the jungle, and the enemy was lobbing mortars at us, hoping for a direct hit on one of the fuel bladders. We responded with a barrage of machine gun fire that ripped through the jungle. I shot several grenades into the countryside with the M-79. The first two were long, but the third landed just past the shoreline. It never occurred to me to pick up a camera.

When the noise subsided, I peered over the sandbags and could see no activity at the shoreline. There were moments of quiet and then someone on one of the boats would fire a quick burst into the jungle, which caused other soldiers to start shooting. A voice from below authoritatively yelled at everyone to stop firing. It would get quiet for a few seconds, until someone fired off another burst and the noise erupted again. This went on for about five minutes after we passed the ambush site.

Nobody on our side was hurt, and none of the LCMs were seriously damaged, so we chugged on upriver. We stopped to unload some fuel at a depot that was located near a small village. The fuel transfer would take a few hours so when a couple of soldiers invited me to visit an opium den, I agreed.

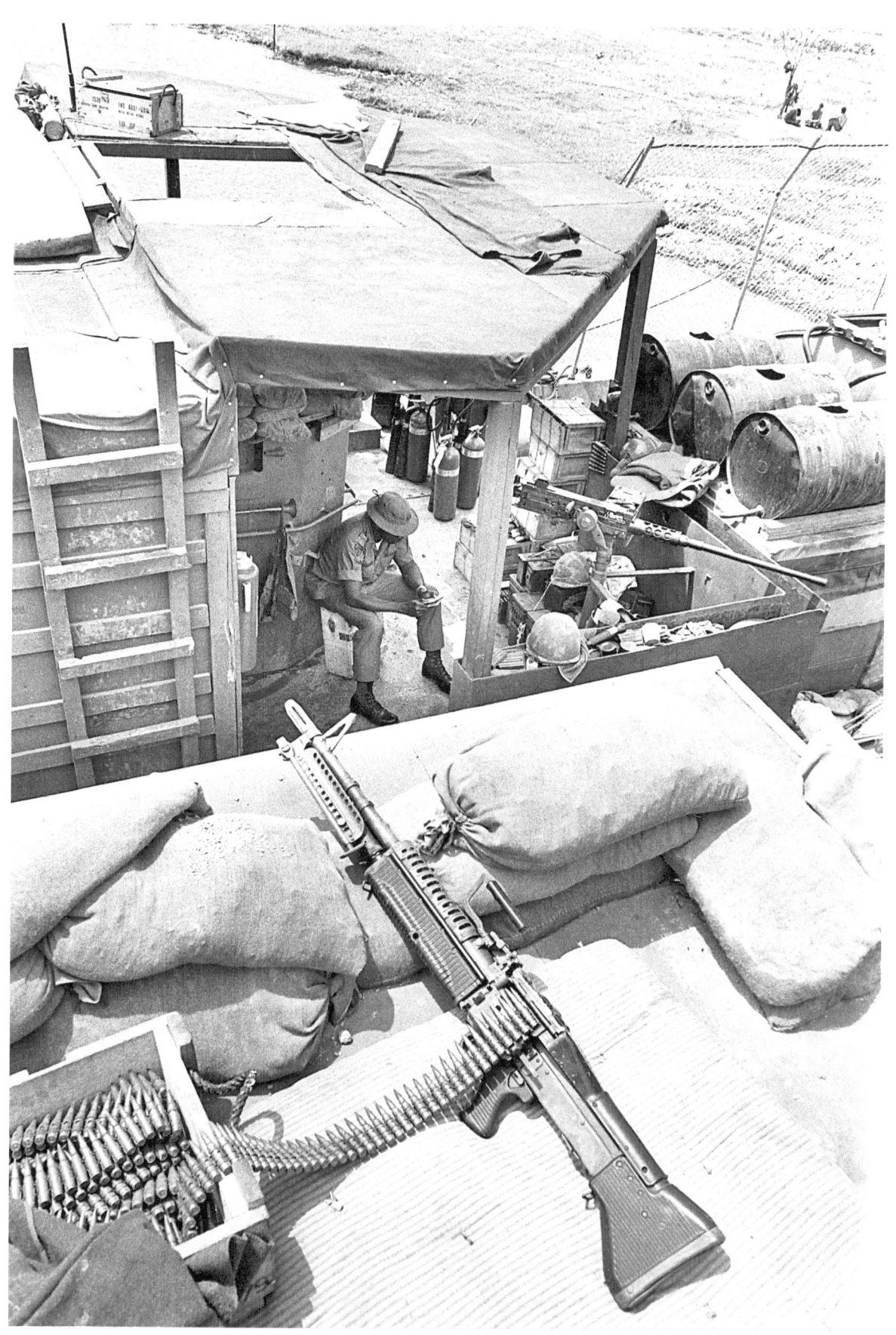

The opium den was not what I expected. It was located inside a carpentry shop where children were playing in the sawdust, and a couple of men with rudimentary hand tools were piecing together a small boat. We gave some money to a woman at the back of the shop and she showed us through a cloth partition, into a dimly lit room.

Against one wall was a low platform with a couple of pillows and a man lying on his side, staring into an oil burning lamp.

There were no introductions or acknowledgments. One of my acquaintances lay down facing the lamp and watched as the man worked a ball of opium onto a pin and passed it across the flame until its consistency was just right. Then he held the smoking ball under the bowl of an inverted pipe and the soldier inhaled its fumes through a flexible stem. We all took turns at the pipe and practically floated back to the boats, stopping once to admire a shrine along the way.

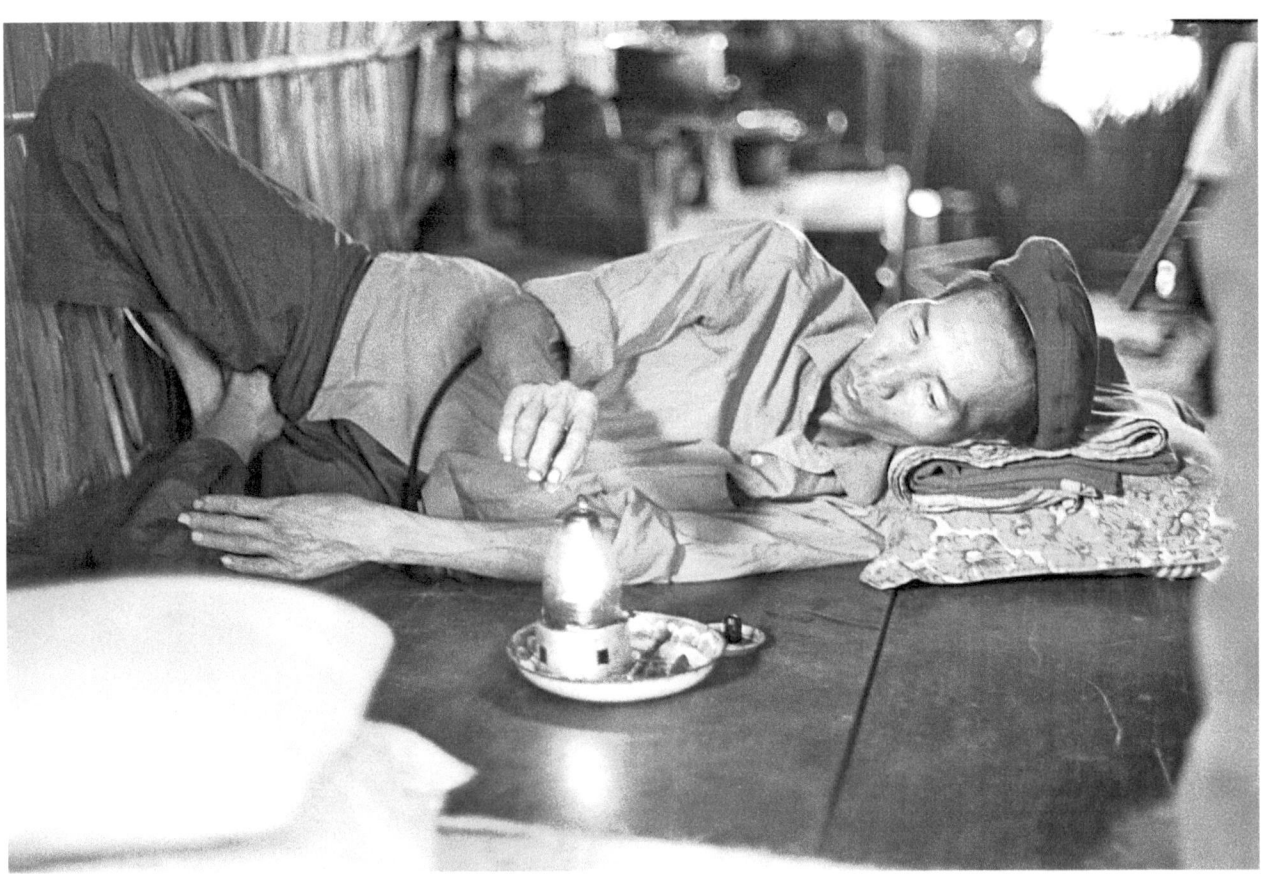

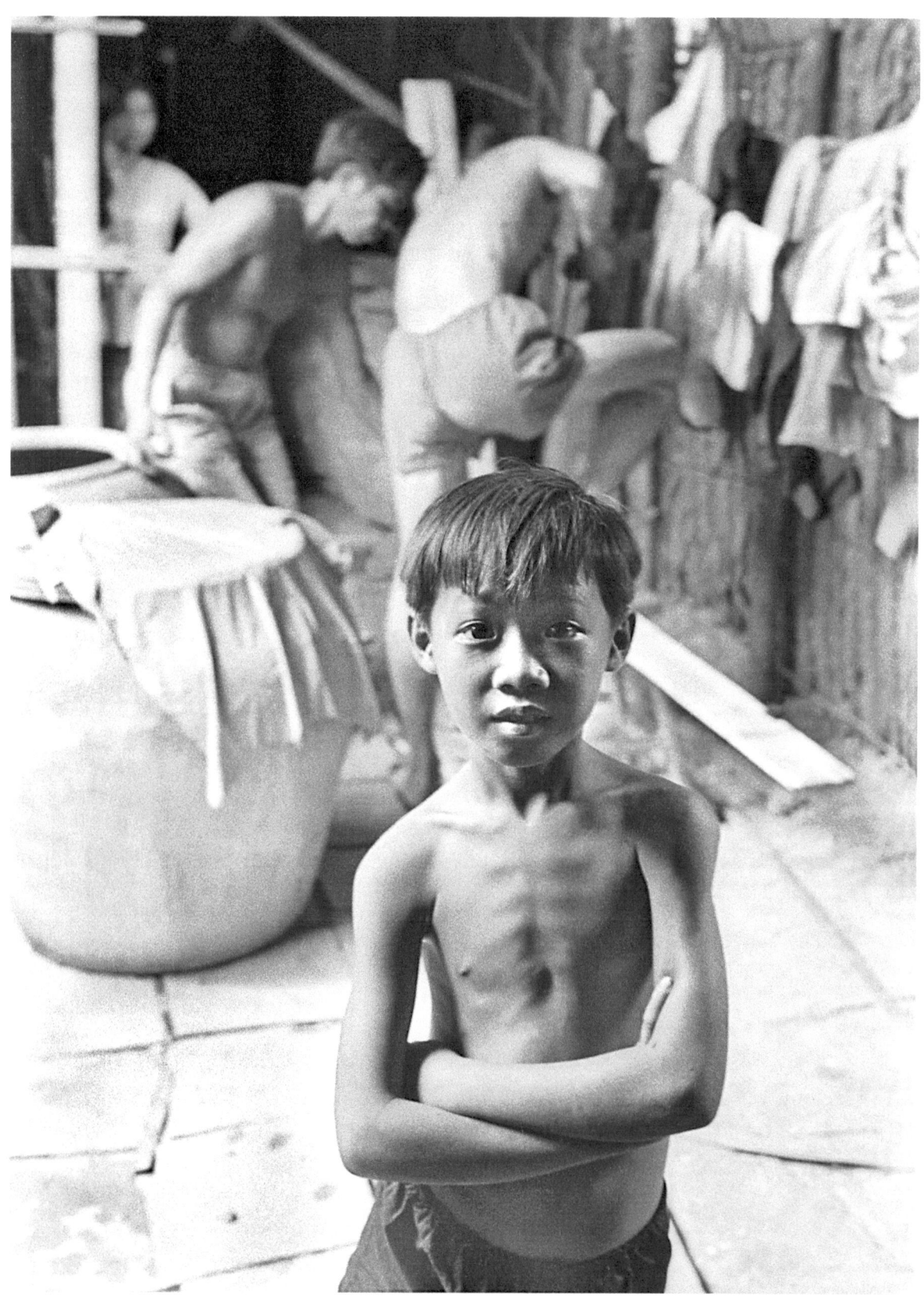

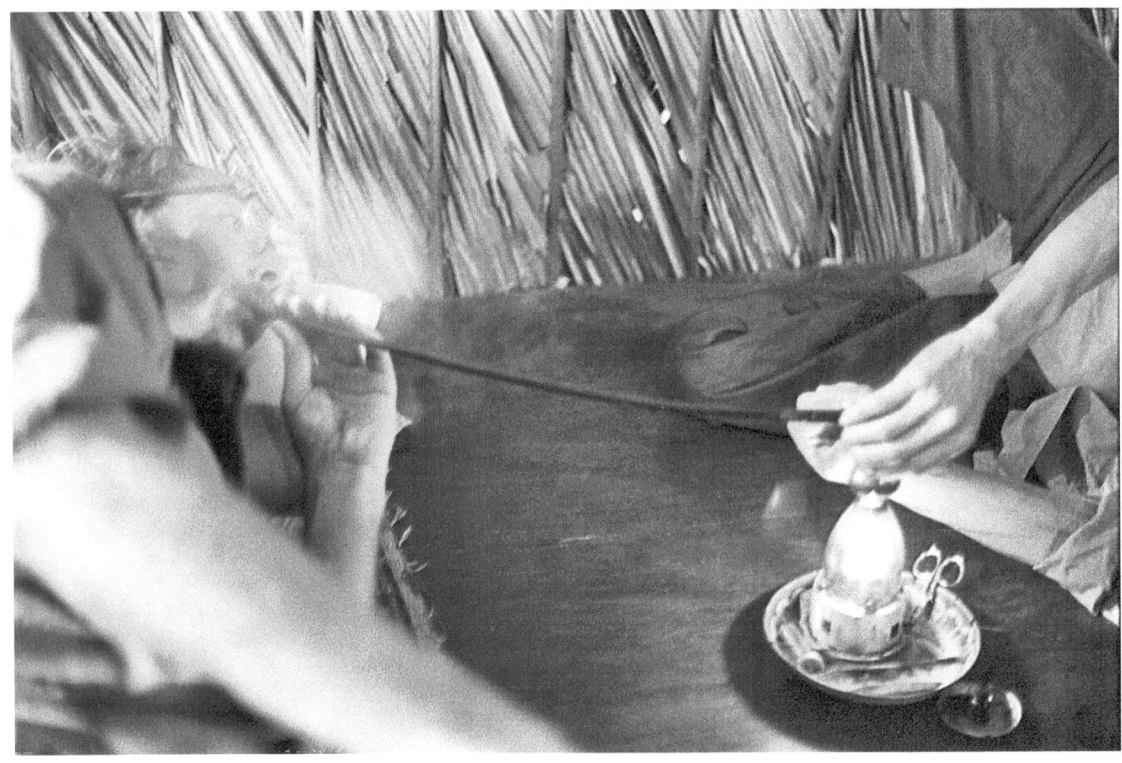

Later that evening and farther upriver I began to lose my equilibrium. I started throwing up and my legs felt as if they could no longer support my weight. I thought the opium man had poisoned me but a medic diagnosed me as malarial.

The convoy dropped me off at the next fueling station where I caught an Air America flight back to Tan Sanute Air Base and eventually ended up in the Long Binh hospital.

That was my last assignment outside of Long Binh. American involvement in Vietnam was winding down. "Vietnamization" of the war was in effect. We were giving it back to its rightful owners. Several months later I received an "early out" to go back to college.

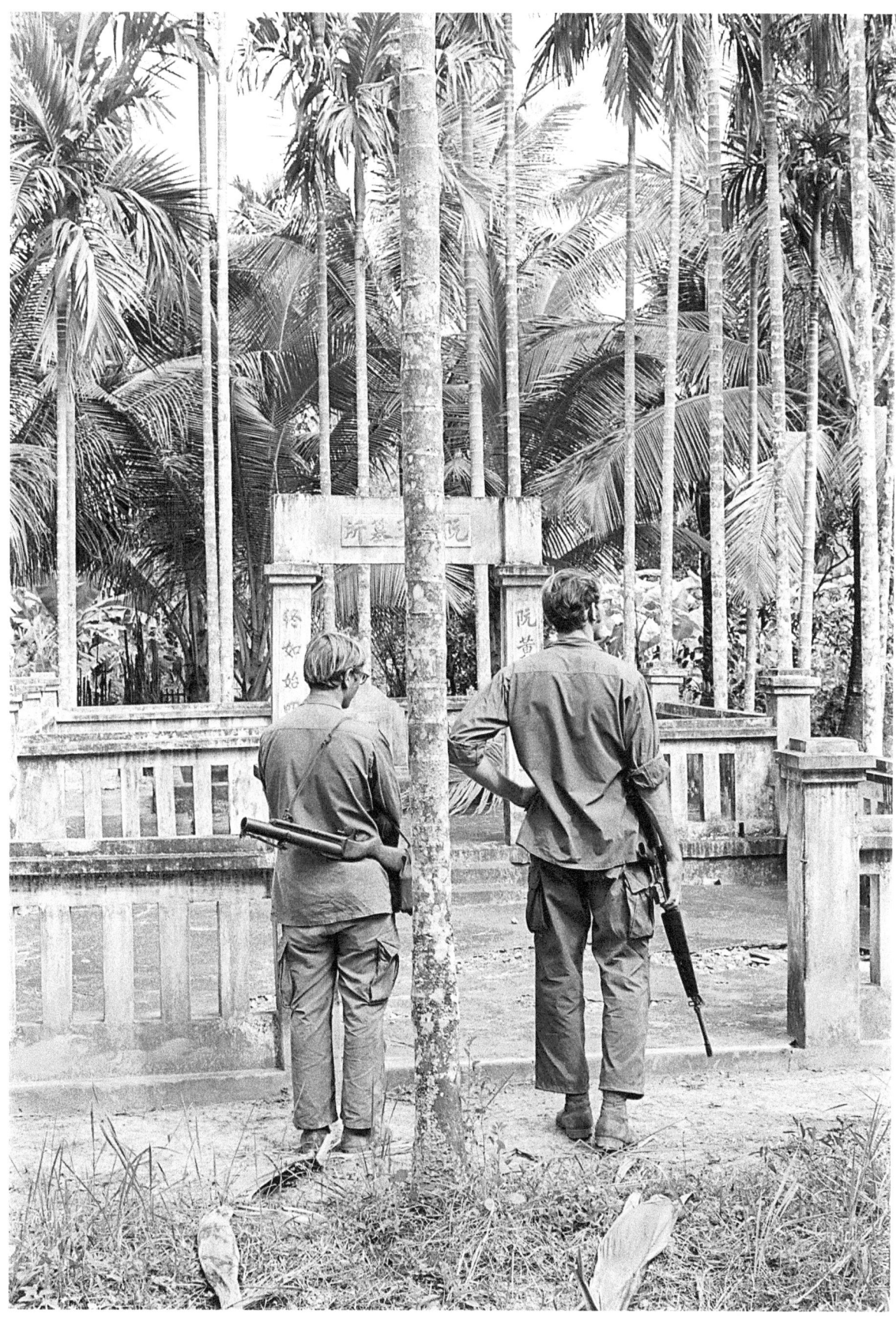

On its journey through Southeast Asia the Mekong River is a chocolate colored ribbon that separates Laos and Thailand, then cuts through the heart of Cambodia and the tip of South Vietnam. It is a highway, a source of income, and a toilet for millions of people.

Inside Vietnam, the Mekong and another river, the Bassic, vein into the delta region where most of the country's rice is grown. Except during monsoon season, the air in this part of Vietnam is hot and heavy.

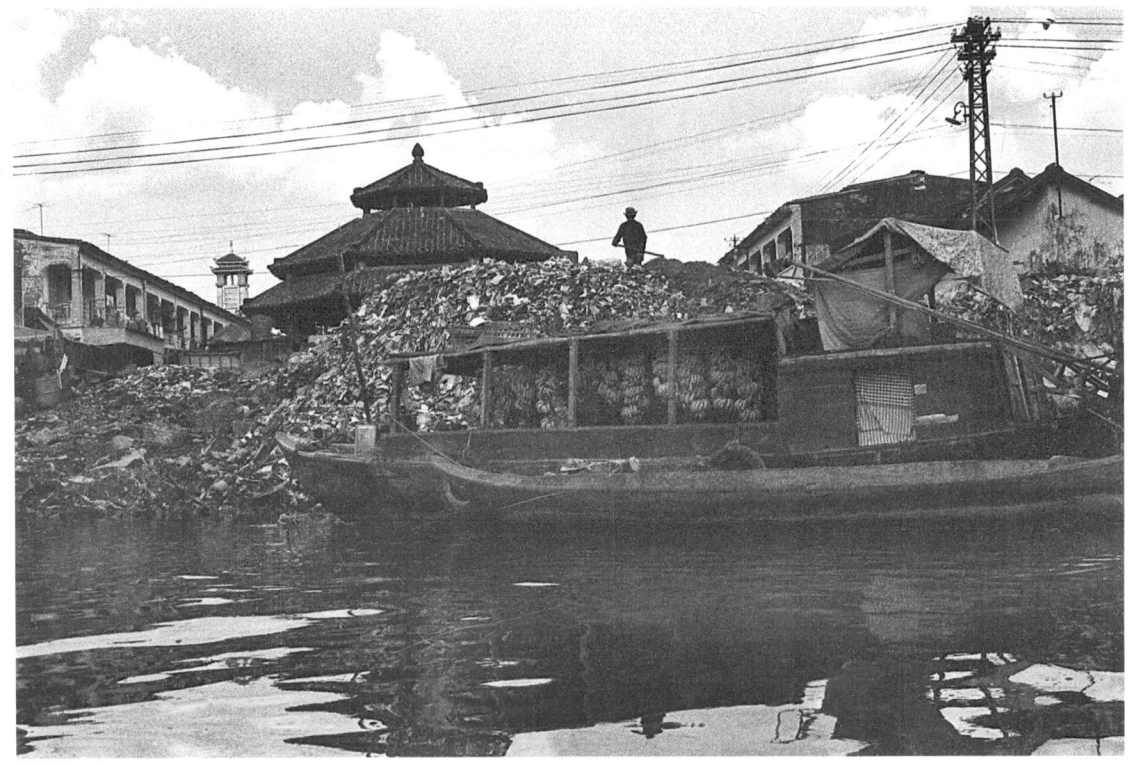

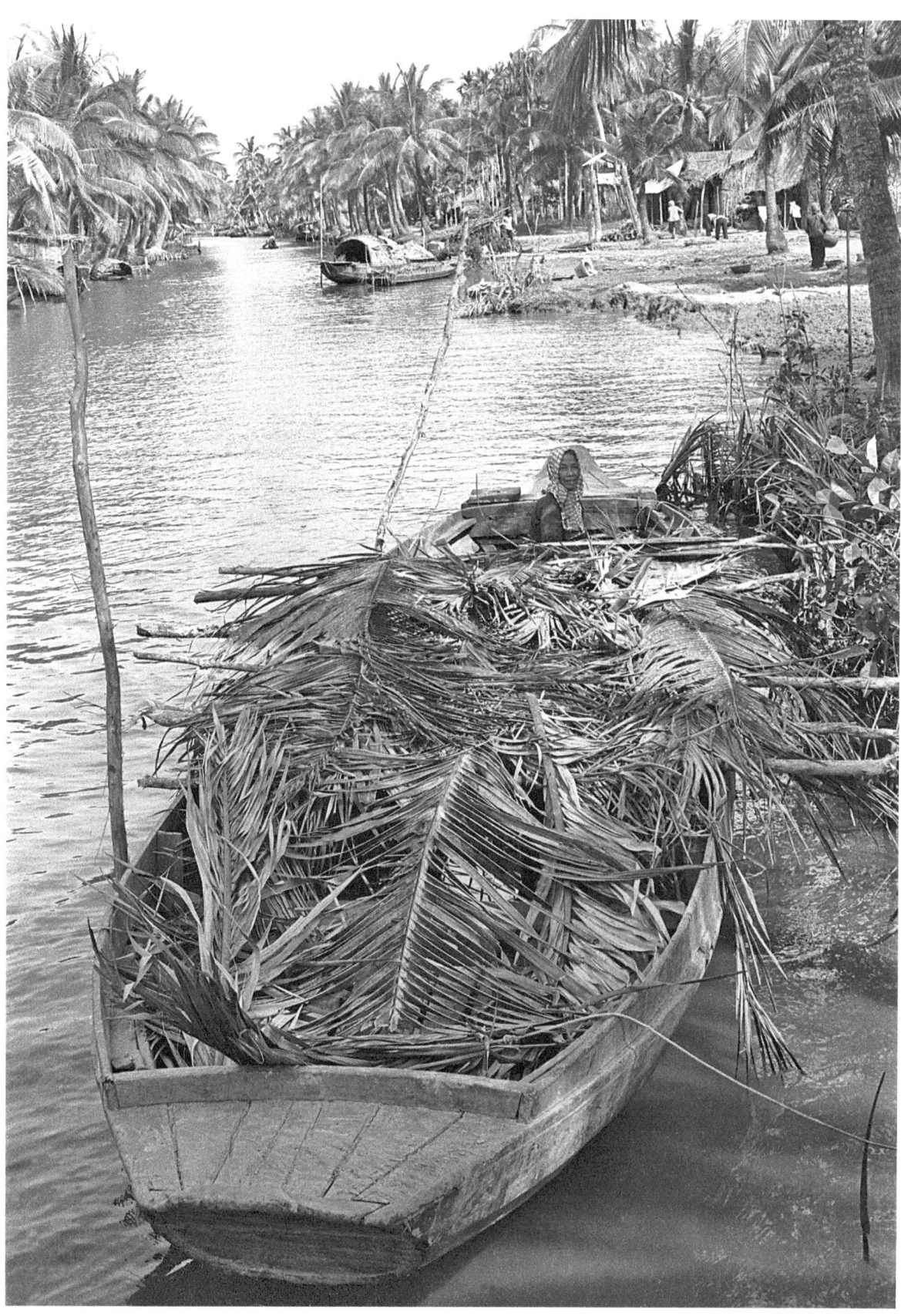

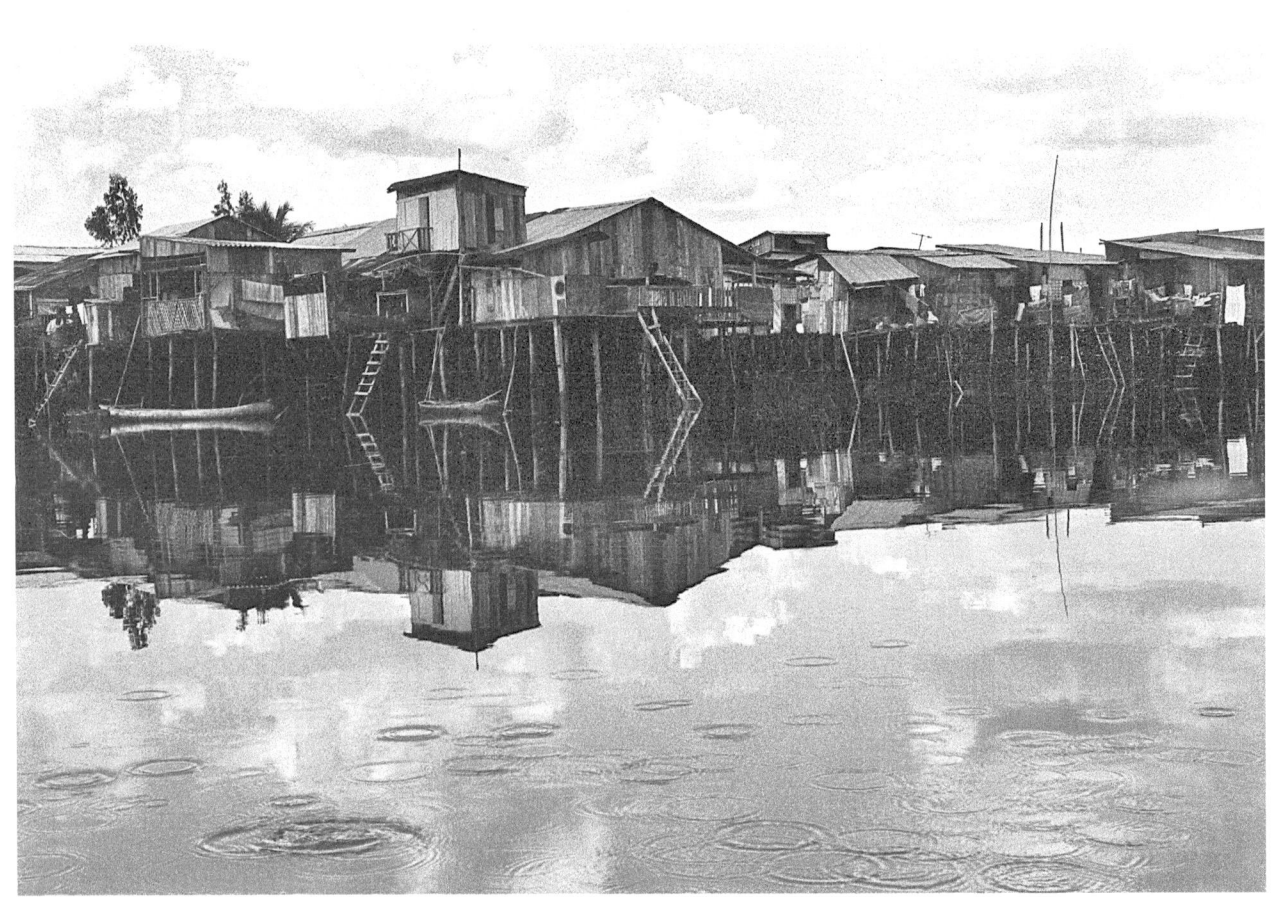

    In the capitol of South Vietnam I took a couple of boat rides on the Saigon River. It was easy to flag down a small motorboat and pay the driver for a trip through the back canals and stilt house neighborhoods.

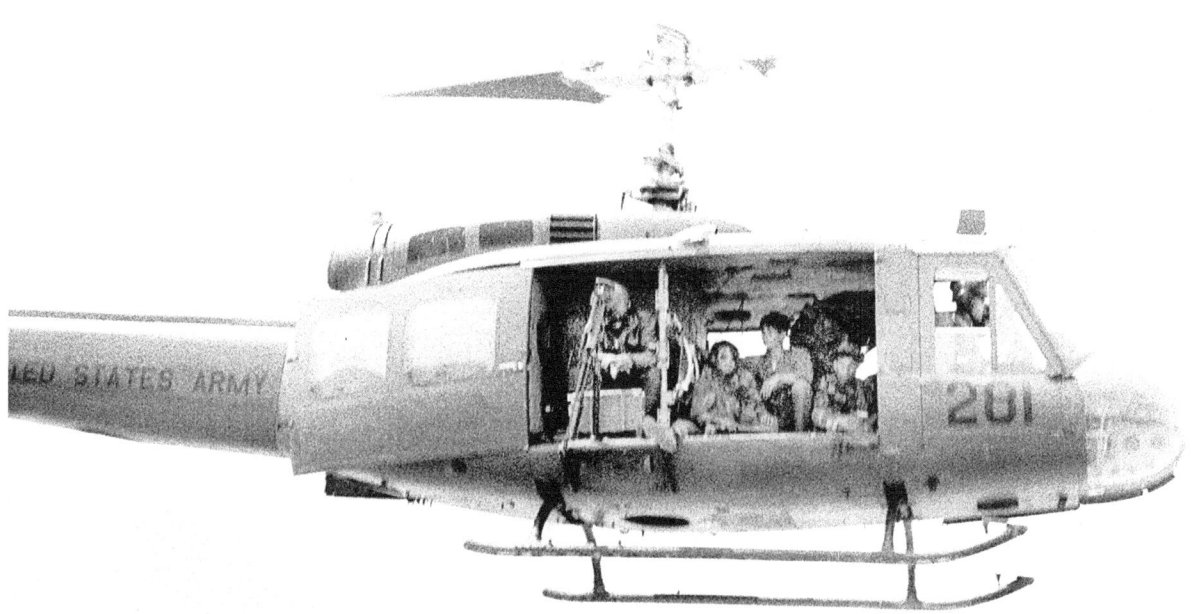

Water and air were places of refuge, so boats and helicopters probably seemed more recreational than they should have. The fact that I never took part in an air assault, and never saw a hot L.Z. had a lot to do with that. I was on a boat that was strafed with machine gun fire, but for some reason the distance from my position to the jungle added an unreasonable sense of safety. Both machines were tethered to the war in the sense that either could be blown out of its element, but that fact never dampened my enthusiasm for leaving the mainland.

Most of my helicopter rides were in Huey slicks, but I do have fond memories of sitting on the floor of a Chinook with my legs dangling out of the opening that the winch line goes through. As the chopper rose, the ground beneath my feet grew more and more distant until the rice paddies and the bomb craters were just abstract patterns that slid in and out of view through the opening. And the air was cooler.

I also caught a few flights on fixed wing aircraft that belonged to Air America. On one occasion I boarded a small plane with the most beautiful Vietnamese girl I had ever seen. She was young and elegant in her crème colored aoi dia, and she was nervous. It was probably her first plane ride. When the plane took off, she threw up into the small plastic bag she was clutching, and I watched it fill with bits of rice, and vomit, and some of it spewed onto her dress. I wanted to comfort her, but she was too embarrassed to raise her head for the rest of the flight.

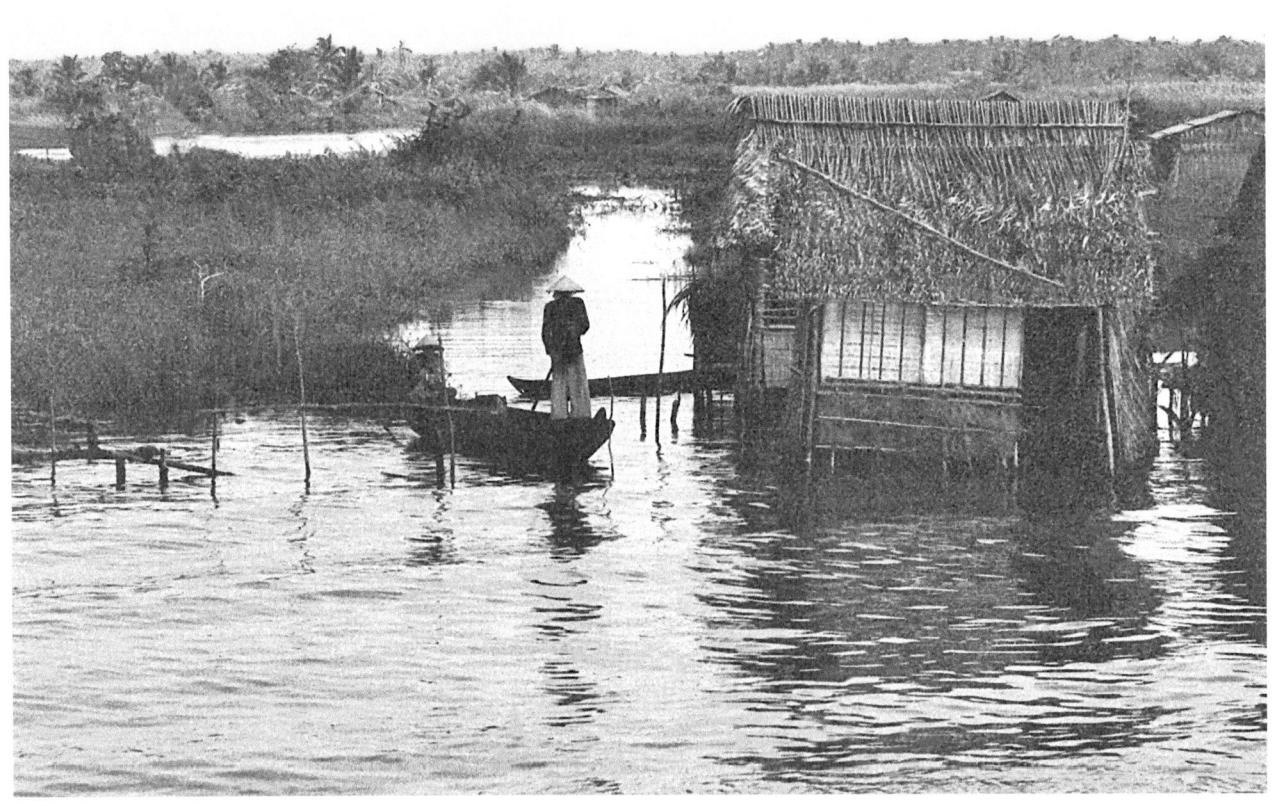

I traveled a short stretch of the Mekong with the Brown Water Navy and watched small boats maneuver through our wake. The boat people in their conical hats rode the river like they were part of it.

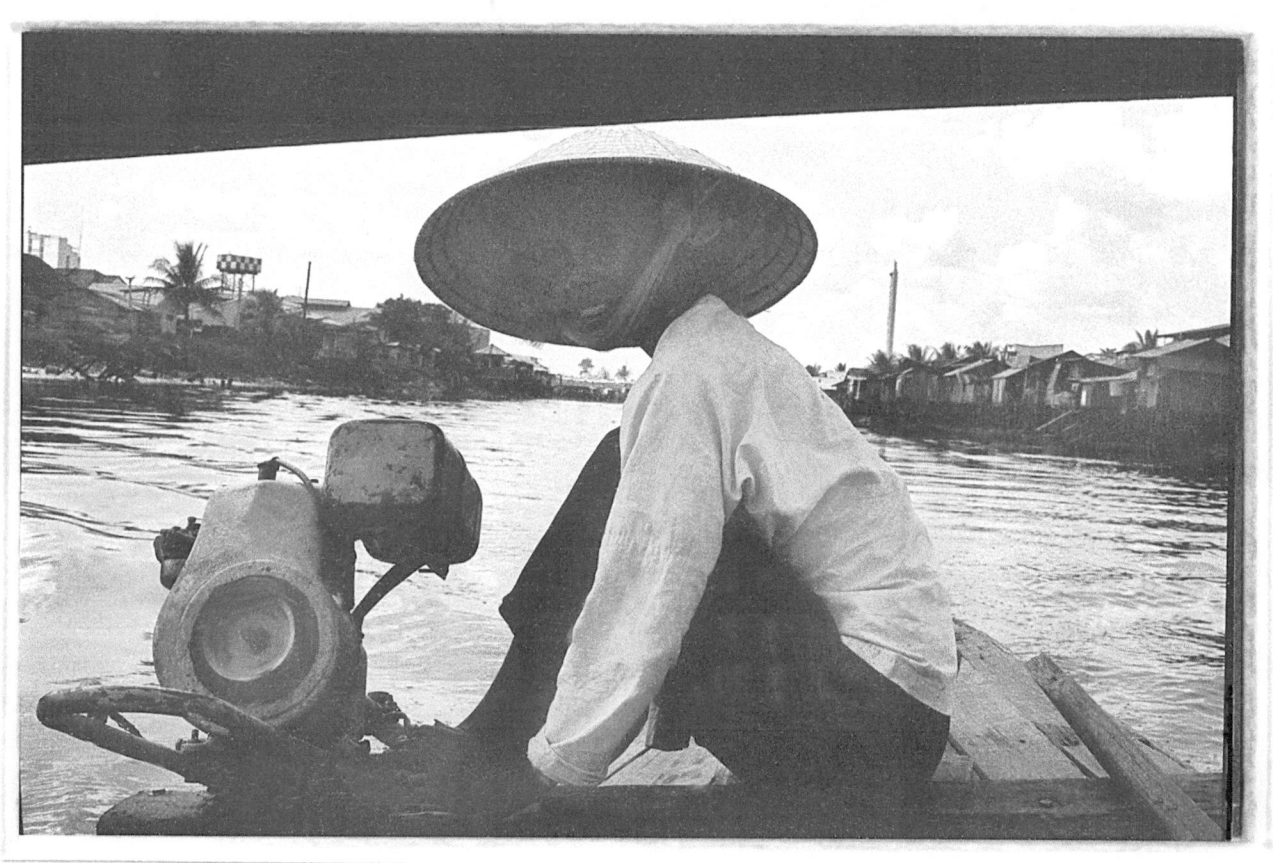

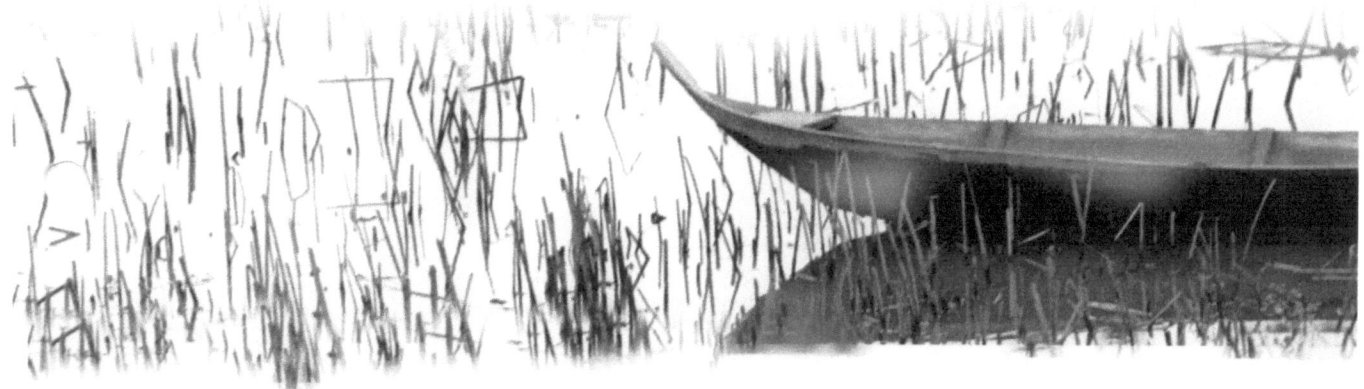

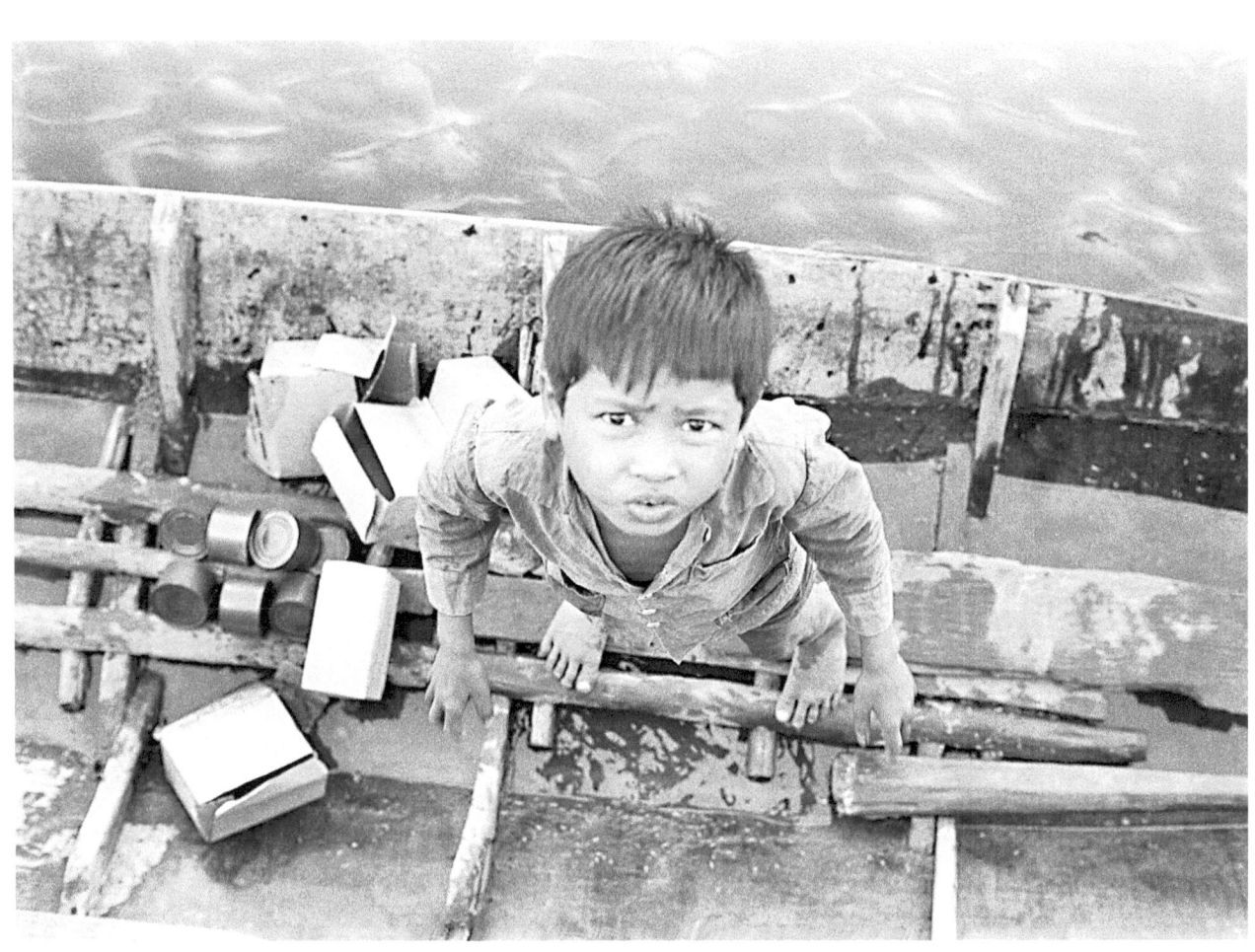

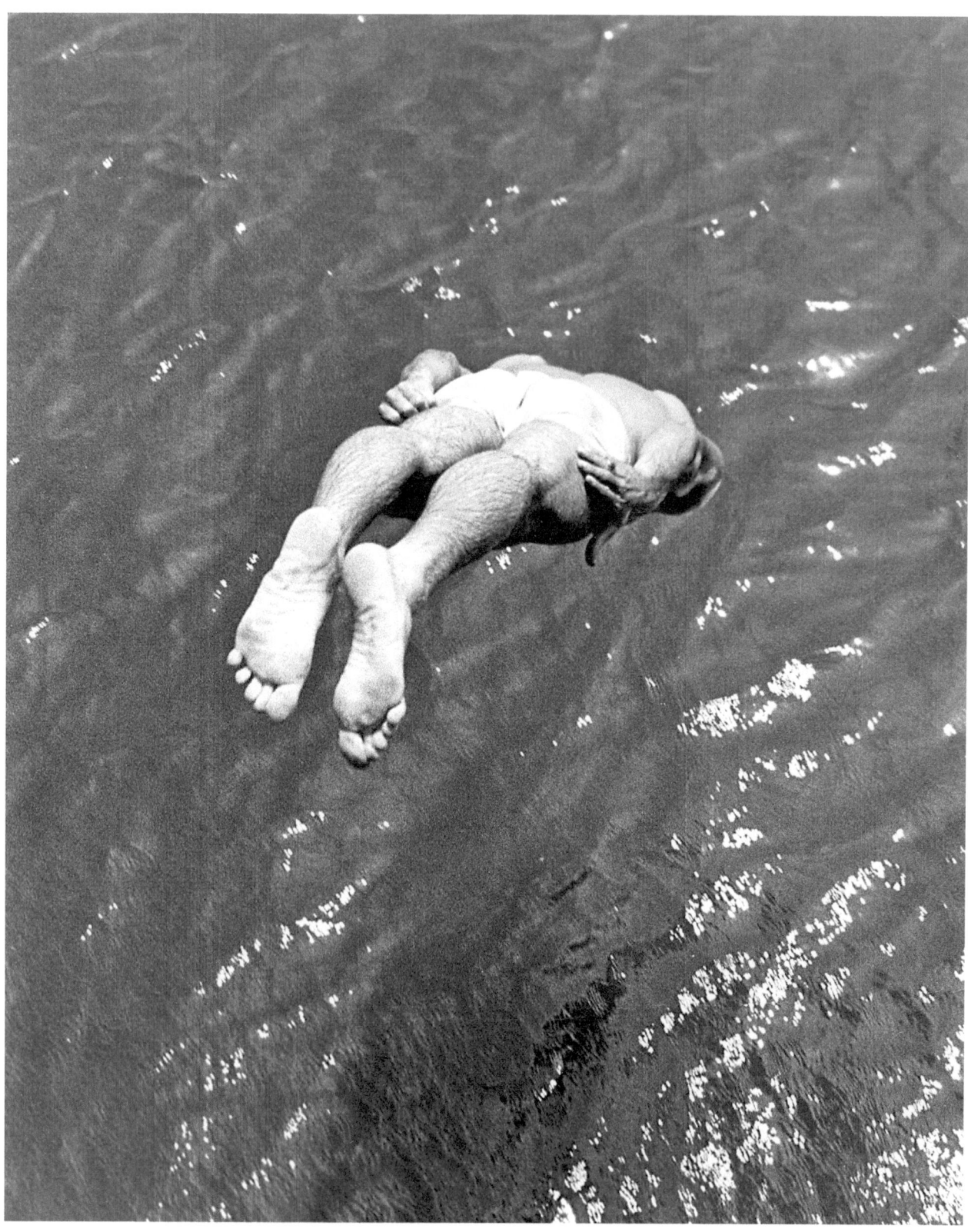

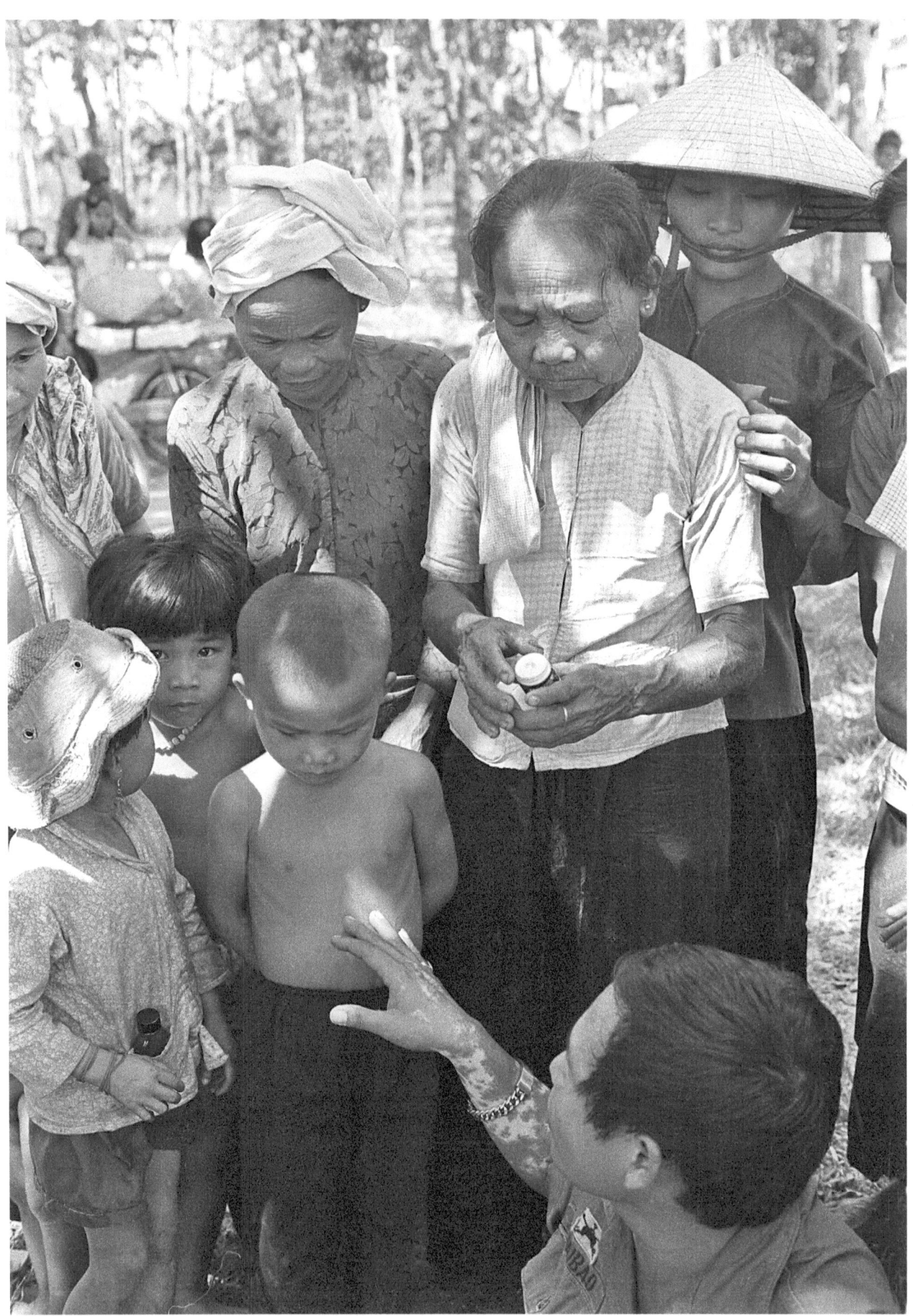

MEDCAP (Medical Civic Action Program) operations were conducted by the 11th Armored Calvary Regiment in the Di An district in 1970. The operations paired US and ARVN medics who treated ailments and dispensed medicine and hygiene advise to Vietnamese civilians.

The medical outings were often conducted in conjunction with PSYOPs, (Psychological Operations), units that interviewed village leaders and evaluated enemy activity in the area.

If PSYOPs personnel were on the scene at this particular occasion, I was not aware of it. I remember the event as a humanitarian excursion where we did something useful for the locals, passed out Red Cross candy to the kids, and left feeling good about ourselves.

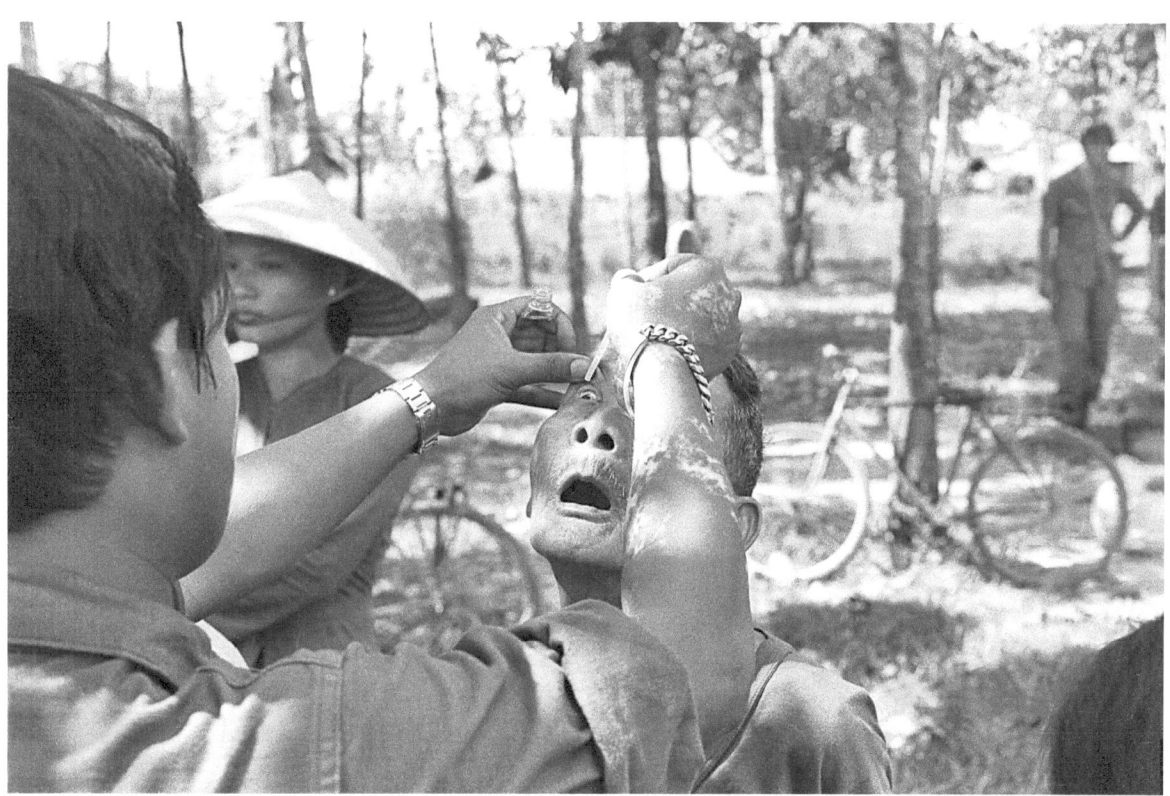

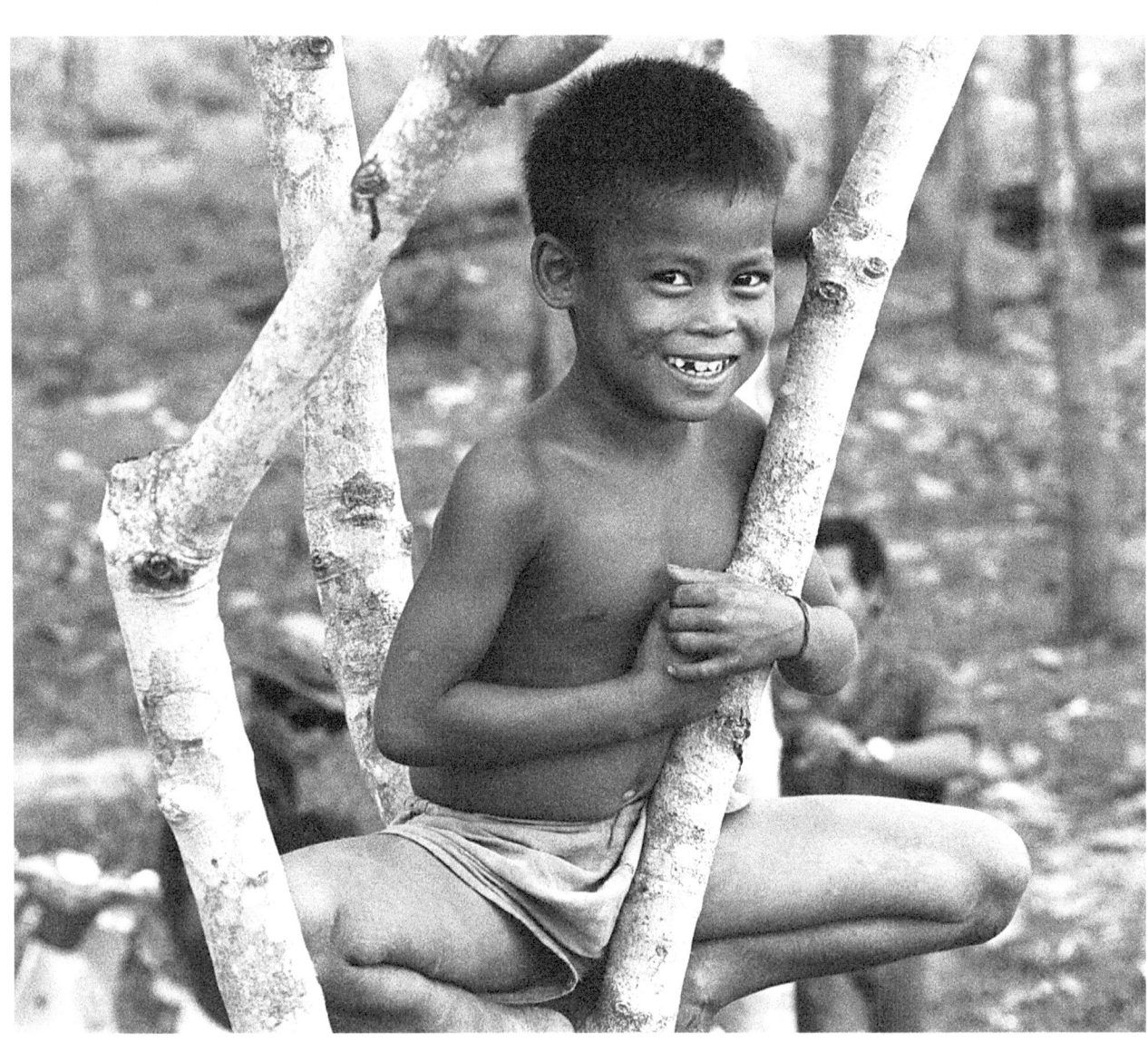

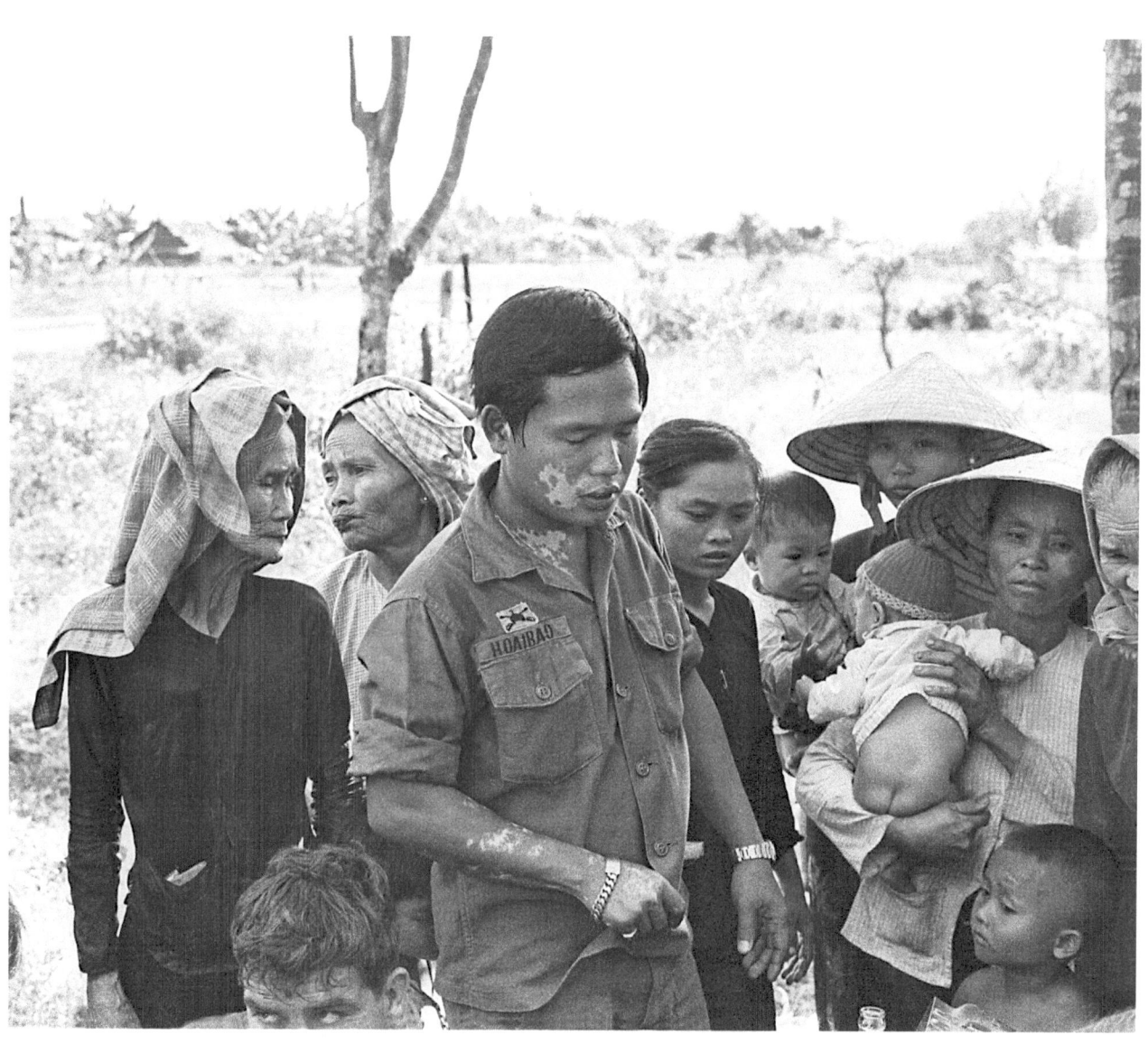

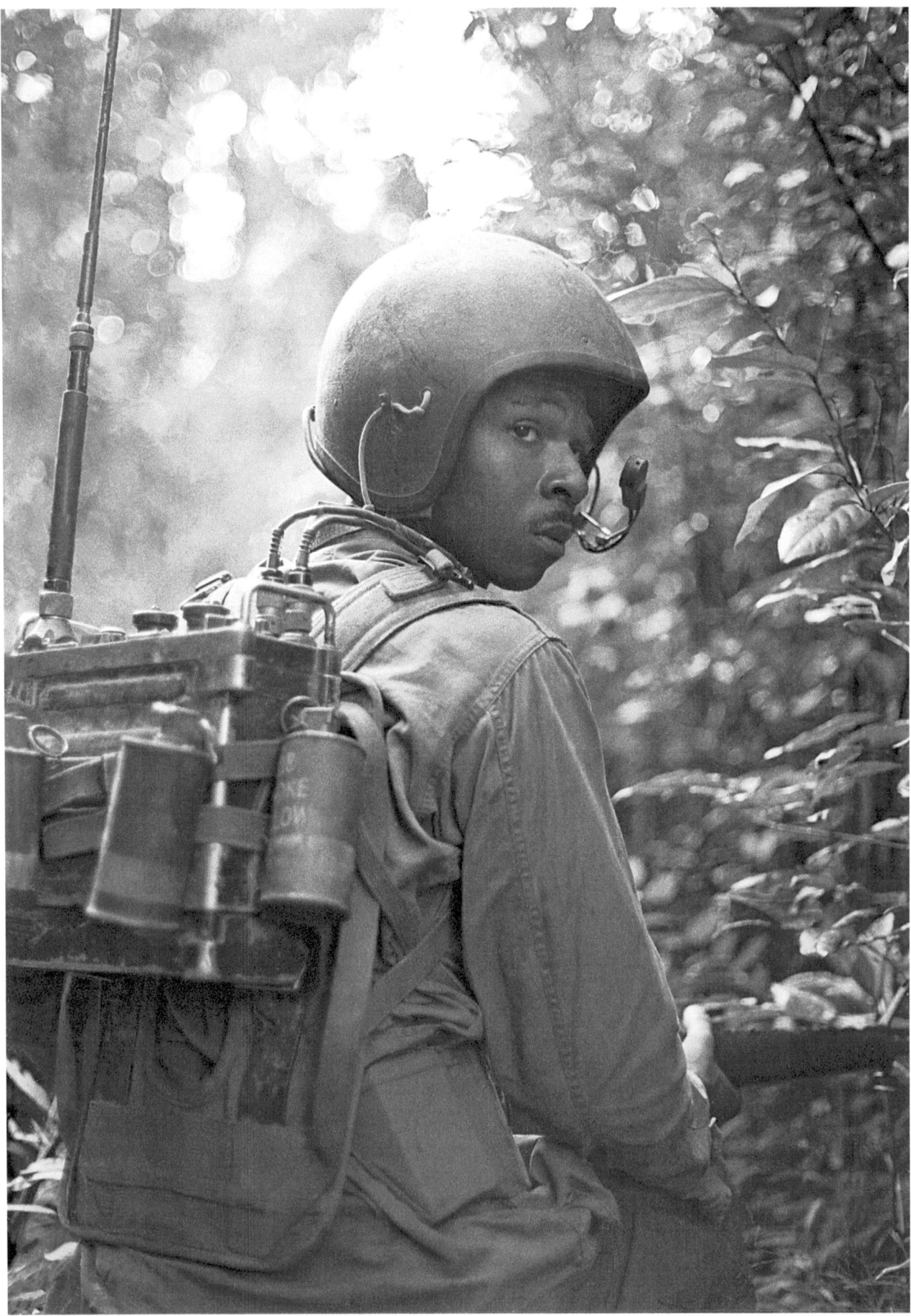

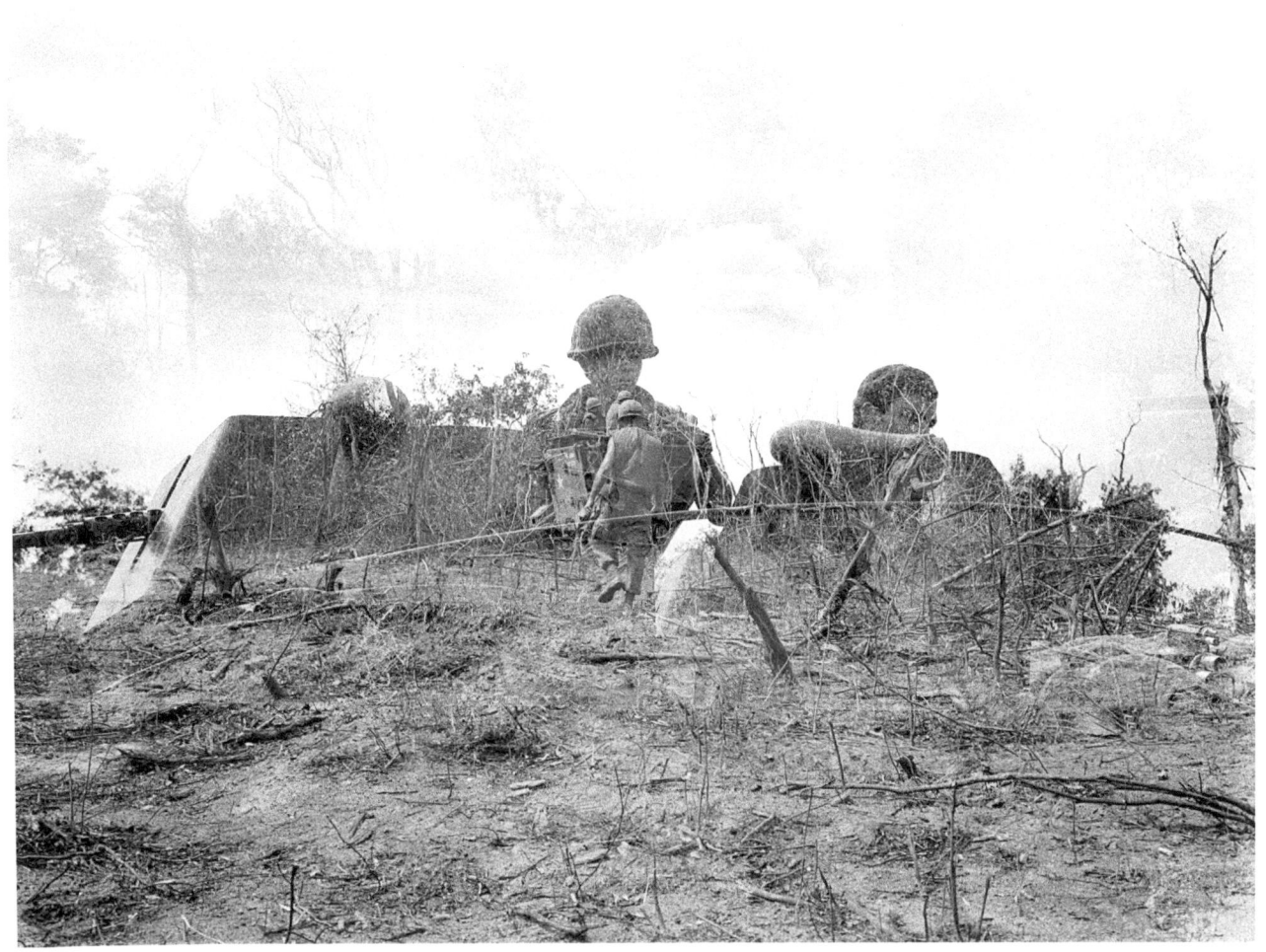

I shot a lot of film in Vietnam—enough to satisfy the Army press corps and myself. And like the Army, I sent my images home, put them in a dark place, and forgot about them for a long time.

www.ingramcontent.com/pod-product-compliance
Lightning Source LLC
Chambersburg PA
CBHW050852180526
45159CB00007B/2654